Global Warming: The Answer

(The Energy Dividend)

by

Wilfred Candler

authorHOUSE®

AuthorHouse™
1663 Liberty Drive, Suite 200
Bloomington, IN 47403
www.authorhouse.com
Phone: 1-800-839-8640

First published by AuthorHouse 10/31/2007

ISBN: 978-1-4343-4508-0 (sc)

Library of Congress Control Number: 2007907934

Printed in the United States of America
Bloomington, Indiana

This book is printed on acid-free paper.

Acronyms

AFCO2TA :	adding fossil carbon dioxide to the atmosphere
AC:	alternating current (transmission line)
ACO2:	atmospheric carbon dioxide
aka:	also known as
ASF:	Atmospheric Stabilization Framework
ASP:	as soon as possible
BAU:	business as usual
bio-carbon:	plant material formed by photosynthesis in recent times.
BTU:	British Thermal Unit
CAT:	Compressed Air Technology
CCS:	Carbon Capture and Sequestration
CDM:	Clean Development Mechanism (Cap and Trade mechanism used by Kyoto and EU)
CEC:	California Energy Commission
CEO:	Chief Executive Officer
CER:	Certified Emission Reduction Credit
CFCs:	chlorofluorocarbons
CFL:	Compact Florescent Lamp
CGE:	Computable General Equilibrium
C&T:	cap-and-trade
CO2:	carbon dioxide
CO2e:	carbon dioxide equivalent (a measure of greenhouse gas concentration)
DC:	direct current
DICE:	Dynamic Integrated model of Climate and the Economy
DOE:	(U.S.) Department of Energy
EDF:	Environmental Defense Fund
EIA:	Energy Information Agency (of DOE)
EIa:	Environmental Investigation Agency (an NGO)

EPA:	(U.S.) Environmental Protection Agency
EPPM:	Emissions Prediction and Policy Model
fossil-carbon:	carbon from coal, oil, natural gas, tar sands, methane hydrate and limestone used for cement production
EU:	European Union
GDP:	Gross Domestic Product
GHG:	Greenhouse Gasses
GTAP:	Global Trade Analysis Project (headquartered at Purdue University).
GtC:	Giga tons of Carbon (1,000,000,000 tons).
GWP:	Global Warming Potential
H20:	water
HCFCs:	hydrochoroflurocarbons
HFCs:	hydrofluorocarbons
HVDC:	high voltage direct current (transmission line)
IGBP:	International Geosphere-Biosphere Program
IGCC:	Integrated Gasification Combined-Cycle
IIASA:	International Institute for Applied Systems Analysis
IMF:	International Monetary Fund
ICMP:	Innovation Comparison Modeling Project
IPCC:	International Panel on Climate Change
MDI:	Moteur Development International
mpg:	miles per gallon
mph:	miles per hour
MIT:	Massachusetts Institute of Technology
MtC:	million metric tons of carbon
NASA:	National Aeronautical and Space Agency
NGO:	non-governmental organization
nimby:	not in my backyard
NO2:	nitrous oxide
NO:	nitrogen oxide

NOAA:	National Oceanographic and Atmospheric Agency
NOx:	nitrous oxide and nitrogen oxide
O2:	oxygen
ORNL:	Oak Ridge National Laboratory
PC:	pulverized coal
PFCs:	perfluorinated compounds
ppm:	parts per million
TAR:	Third Assessment Report (of the IPCC, 2001)
TBD:	to be decided
REC:	Renewable Energy Certificate
RD&D:	Research, Development and Demonstration
RICE:	Regional dynamic Integrated Model of Climate and the Economy.
RPS:	Renewable Portfolio Standard
SRES:	Special Report on Emission Scenarios
SUV:	Sports Utility Vehicle
U.K.:	United Kingdom
UNFCCC:	United Nations Framework Convention on Climate Change
U.S.:	United States of America
USCAP:	United States Climate Action Partnership
USGS:	United States Geological Service
VAT:	value added tax
WG2:	Working Group Two (of the IPCC)
WTO:	World Trade Organization

Contents

Preface

There is now widespread acceptance that by adding fossil carbon dioxide to the atmosphere (AFCO2TA) we are causing global warming[1]. Most forecasts of the impact of global warming are fairly modest and over a substantial time period ("3 foot sea rise by 2100", or "doubling of atmospheric C02 (ACO2) by 2050", and the like), leading to the conclusion that "we have to do something now,….but not today". This conclusion is almost certainly wrong. Global warming is *already having adverse effects*, melting glaciers and permafrost, drowning islands and changing rainfall patterns[2], and *change takes time*. Most cars last ten years, power stations often operate for 50 years, and with current technology and regulation nuclear plants take a decade to build and commission. Many investments made today, are expected to be in use in 2050, if not 2100.

Moreover, there are lags before the full effects of rising ACO2 (atmospheric carbon dioxide) work themselves out. As ACO2 rises, temperature rises, sea-ice melts, and the amount of sunlight reflected into space declines, leading to further warming (one of many possible feed-back loops). Even if we stopped AFCO2TA (adding fossil carbon dioxide to the atmosphere) today warming would continue until a new equilibrium was reached; and despite climate models we can have very little idea as to what the full climatic effects of this temperature rise would be. All that we know is that climate models consistently over-estimate the time that will elapse before effects are felt.

We are already at concentrations of ACO2 well in excess of anything that has been experienced in the last 450,000 years (Figure 1). We are already in uncharted climatic territory, and scientists have known this since 1990.

No one imagines that we can completely stop AFCO2TA (adding fossil carbon dioxide to the atmosphere) in less than a decade, so not only are we committed to the CO2 we have already added to the atmosphere, but also to at least a further decade of additions.

The time to bring down the rate of AFCO2TA (adding fossil carbon dioxide to the atmosphere) is now.

Four misconceptions bedevil much discussion of global warming. The first is that the problem is carbon dioxide (CO2) (or "greenhouse gas") emissions from any source. This equates bio-carbon dioxide emissions from the decay or burning of plants (bio-CO2), with CO2 generated from fossil-carbon (coal, oil, natural gas, tar sands and limestone) (fossil-CO2). The difference is that bio-carbon has recently been *withdrawn* from the atmosphere by photosynthesis in the process of plant growth. Fossil- carbon has been sequestered (out of the carbon cycle) for millions of years. The *return* of bio-CO2 to the atmosphere is fundamental to life, no atmospheric CO2, would mean no plant life and would mean no life as we know it, although a few anaerobic deep ocean heat-vent dependent life forms might survive. *The problem is excessive releases of fossil-CO2 (and associated fossil greenhouse gasses) being* <u>*added*</u> *to the carbon cycle.*

The second misconception is that all we need to do is to reduce the rate of AFCO2TA to some historic level, say the rate in 1990. Ever since the beginnings of the industrial revolution (circa 1850) mankind has been AFCO2TA and ACO2 (atmospheric CO2) concentrations have risen steadily year by year. *To begin to stabilize global temperatures we have to stop* (not reduce the rate of) *AFCO2TA*[3].

A third misconception is that global warming is a technological problem: "We have to develop fossil-free energy sources". No! *Global warming is an economic problem: "We have to establish price signals that will lead people to no longer use fossil based energy* and that will lead venture capitalists to invest in the development of new sources of fossil-free energy".

A fourth misconception (rapidly disappearing) is that there is uncertainty as to the existence of global warming, and/or its likely impact. Some have even pushed that global warming could be beneficial due to CO2-fertilization of plants[4]. *This uncertainty has been conscientiously fostered by leading energy companies via their contributions to the Global Climate Coalition*, the Enterprise Institute and other front organizations. Like the manufacturers of asbestos this support may eventually prove very costly, as legal suits based on damage caused by global warming are addressed to deep pocket companies. Some of these same companies have recently regrouped using the Environmental Defense Fund and other environmental NGOs[5] in a new organization, *US Climate Action Partnership* (USCAP) to promote cap-and-trade: *This should be an early warning that cap-and-trade is not a good policy.*

Parallel with global warming, there is an associated economic fear of "The Oil Peak", the year when world petroleum production will reach its highest point, with all later years yielding lower production. Catastrophe scenarios are woven of mounting demand for oil meeting declining supply, with rapid price rises and "physical" shortages of petrol. It is easy to envisage the economy grinding to a halt as gas stations dry up, stranded motorists, complete break-down of the supply chain, etc. However, if we take global warming seriously and understand that it will be climatically catastrophic to continue AFCO2TA, *we need to stop using fossil fuels even before they run out.* The Oil-Peak literature enables us to visualize the potential economic and political disruptions likely to be involved in our overdue retreat from the carbon economy. The whole trick (to which this book is addressed) will be to rapidly reduce our reliance on fossil fuels but in a way that is not too economically damaging.

A hazard in writing this book, has been how rapidly the debate on global warming, and evidence of its impact is advancing. It is almost to the point that every day brings something that would ideally involve elaboration of a point, or even whole new sections in the book. One of the key books on global warming is called "Field Notes from a Catastrophe", writing this book has felt more like "Field Notes *During* a Catastrophe".

As this book was going to press, Congressman John Dingell, Chairman of the House Energy and Commerce Committee, has final introduced legislation to tax carbon (at $10 a ton in the first year, rising to $50 in the fifth year, as compared with the book's recommendation of $250 a ton immediately). He also would return some of the revenue to tax-payers by increasing the earned income credit, while reserving a balance for good causes. This again falls well short of our recommendation to return the entire take as an energy dividend to all registered voters, but in these troubled times we must be thankful for any apparent allies. Certainly the Congressman is to be congratulated for not falling for the cap-and-trade boondoggle.

Numerous organizations and individual have generously allowed me to use their illustrations and arguments: I find it encouraging to know that others share my concerns. In this connection I would like to thank the Estate of Karl Davies, Dr. James Hansen, Jamie Hartzell, Michael D. Mastrandrea, S. Schneider, U.S. Department of Energy, U.K. Treasury, Oak Ridge National Laboratory, National Oceanic and Atmospheric Administration, IPCC, California Energy Commission, San Francisco Chronicle, the New York Times (for quotations of two sentences or less), American Public Media, passivhaus, Annual Review of Energy and the Environment, the Transnational Institute, carbonwatch.org, Green-e.org, econobusinesslinks.com, Environmental Resources Trust, Precision Combustion Inc. and zfacts.com.

I would like to acknowledge the helpful assistance of Wayne Cartwright, Ross Gelbspan and especially my wife, Margaret, who forced me into writing this book.

Introduction

The question addressed in this book is: *Given a decision by a nation, state, province or city to stop adding fossil carbon dioxide to the atmosphere (AFCO2TA): How can they do this at least cost/ maximum benefit to the citizens or voters?* It is worth noting, that China and the United States are currently responsible for about sixteen percent (each) of fossil carbon dioxide emissions. If either of them stopped adding fossil CO2 to the atmosphere, they could drop such additions by 16 percent globally, or working together by about 32 percent. Clearly these economies cannot hide behind the argument that they are too small to make a noticeable difference. It would have a noticeable effect on global warming if the United States eliminated its fossil emissions, *even if no other country made any changes.*

China and the United States are the leading polluters, China having passed the United States in 2006 by releasing 6.2 billion tons of CO2 (1.68 billion m tons of carbon), versus 5.8 billion tons of CO2 (1.58 billion tons of carbon) by the United States[6]. The U.S. (and China) are such large scale polluters, that if they achieved zero emissions, this would reduce significantly reduce *global* emissions.

A first chapter focuses on the difference between *fossil-carbon* that has been sequestered for millions of years, and *bio-carbon* that has recently been withdrawn from the atmosphere by photosynthesis. This is a crucial distinction since many discussions of global warming do not adequately (if at all) distinguish between fossil- and bio-carbon. This chapter also points to the period for which bio-carbon is typically sequestered, depending whether it is sequestered in an annual, shrub or tree; and the difference between current and accumulated fossil-carbon emissions. From this discussion it follows that *any program to reduce global warming* needs to discourage AFCO2TA (adding fossil carbon dioxide to the atmosphere). Readers already familiar with these concepts may wish to skip to Chapter 2.

The second chapter focuses on global warming as an *economic problem*: *Get the prices right and the technology will follow*. In particular the problem of "market failure": The benefits of using cheap fossil energy go to the user, while the costs are born by everyone; and especially the difficulty of negotiating international agreements in the presence of market failure (where prices are giving the wrong signals). The chapter also discusses the difficulty of forecasting/modeling future climate change, when this is expected to take us beyond the range of properly documented historical experience. Again, the reader familiar with these concepts may wish to skip to Chapter 3.

The third chapter deals with what Vice-President Cheney has described as the "personal virtue" of modifying ones lifestyle so as to minimize fossil carbon emissions (or even to minimize energy use in general). These changes are important (not least to the feeling of self-worth for the individual involved) and we have to rely on some personal virtue beyond what is indicated by price signals. Personal virtue does not necessitate reducing carbon emissions, provided that bio-carbon is substituted for fossil-carbon wherever possible. Illustrative life-style changes are discussed. Unfortunately personal virtue alone is unlikely to solve the problem of global warming.

The fourth chapter examines the concept of a "carbon neutral" lifestyle, where this is achieved not by modifications of personal behavior, but by buying "carbon credits" to offset actual fossil-carbon releases by the individual involved. It is shown that carbon credits have as little to do with limiting AFCO2TA, as Medieval Indulgences had to do with limiting sin. Rather they are taken to be a permit for the buyer to AFCO2TA. Already selling carbon credits, of doubtful providence, is a $100 million industry. It is argued that this is in fact a "feel-good" lifestyle that cannot be relied upon to achieve even the modest reductions in AFCO2TA that can be achieved by personal virtue. Readers tempted "to do their bit" by buying carbon credits to achieve a "carbon neutral" lifestyle are urged not to skip this chapter.

The fifth chapter looks at the chimera of "clean coal" and the hope of finding "pollution free" technologies to allow the continued use of fossil fuels; the American idea of achieving "energy independence" by using coal to produce gasoline; and a dangerous interest in using the inexhaustible supply of methane hydrates to substitute for natural gas.

The sixth chapter addresses the currently most popular proposals for limiting AFCO2TA, namely *"cap-and-trade"*. The problem with cap-and-trade is that it gives established polluters a free-ride at least up to the level of their cap. It could thus perhaps be described as the (established) *Polluters Protection Program*. It is significant that some of the key supporters of the Global Climate Coalition (that was dedicated to discrediting even the existence of global warming) have reorganized as a lobby (US Climate Action Partnership, USCAP) promoting cap-and-trade; *this fact alone should be sufficient to throw doubt on the wisdom of this policy.*

The seventh chapter provides "the answer", namely an "energy dividend" payable to all voters, and financed by the revenues from a carbon tax. This works like cap-and-trade would with a zero cap for everyone, and the government (national, state or local) as the only vendor of carbon credits. The result is that the government (rather than established polluters) gets the revenue from carbon credits. This revenue from the fossil-carbon tax can be redistributed to the citizenry to help offset the higher cost of living resulting from the carbon tax. Consumers would pay more for fossil based power (as they would under cap-and-trade) but can be compensated with a monthly government "energy dividend". These are fairly complicated ideas, and are spelt out in greater detail in the chapter. If you are going to skip this chapter, you should not have bought the book. Should sequestration of CO_2 collected from the atmosphere prove to be technically and economically feasible, then the above policies would need to be reconsidered to take proper advantage of possibility of actually reducing ACO2.

The eighth chapter discusses modifications to "the answer", it shows that there is a continuum of policies from cap-and-trade to a revenue neutral fossil-carbon tax, and between the energy dividend and an (apparently still born) British proposal to give tradable carbon caps to individual consumers.

The ninth chapter describes some of the major investments that will be needed to replace the legacy *alternating current electric* grid designed to cope with varying demand for electricity, to a new *direct current grid* able to adjust demand to varying supplies of electricity from wind-farms and solar sources.

The tenth chapter deals briefly with the nitrogen cycle, terrestrial ozone, and industrial greenhouse gasses, particularly the man-made fluorocarbons.

The eleventh chapter explores the vexed question of how to reach international agreement on the control of ACO2 emissions, when many countries still believe that cheap energy is crucial to their economic prosperity, and when there is no agreed basis for setting fair and equitable national limits on emissions. Strangely there may here be a role for the WTO (World Trade Organization) that already rules on the technologies acceptable for the production of internationally traded goods.

The twelfth chapter sets out a detailed multi-pronged action program in line with "the answer", since the author is sick and tired of being told that "we have just another decade to make tough choices" with nary a hint as to why the tough decisions can be delayed for a decade, or what these tough decisions might be.

The thirteenth Chapter discusses recent testimony by Dr. James Hansen, to the House Select Committee on the Environment and Global Warming. It compares and contrasts his policy prescriptions with those already discussed.

The fourteenth chapter "Spaceship Titanic", points to a notable lack of political leadership at the highest levels, under-funded and miss-directed research, muzzling of government scientists, counter-productive dilettante "environmentalists" whose opposition to wind farms and nuclear plants puts the whole planet at risk, "chicken little" environmentalists who tell us (quite rightly) that the oceans are rising, but fail to tell us how to mend our ways, the absence of in-depth reporting by the media, and a general public so trusting, that they will be genuinely surprised when we hit an iceberg and discover that there are not enough lifeboats.

The final chapter "Keeping Tabs" provides a "do it yourself" method of keeping month by month tabs on how we are doing. It provides a "poor man's 'reduced form' IPCC model" of ACO2 concentrations under "business as usual" (BAU) where ACO2 concentrations follow a linear, quadratic or cubic curve fitted to Moana Loa ACO2 data from 1958 to date. The seven of the first eight months of 2007 have had ACO2 levels above the BAU curve, suggesting that far from bringing ACO2 concentrations under control, the rate of AFCO2TA (perhaps augmented by positive feed-back loops leading to an increased proportion of bio-carbon being in ACO2) is increasing even faster than it has for the last 50 years.

In reviewing the literature, it is disappointing to find that key ideas as discussed in Chapter 7 *the answer* *have been known since at least 1992*[7]:

"One major by-product of charge systems is a flow of financial resources from polluters to the government. This financial transfer can be substantial; the Congressional Budget Office estimates $100 per ton on carbon dioxide (CO2) ($ 367.00 per ton of carbon) emissions (to address global climate change) could result in more than $120 billion in annual revenues to the government. This raises the obvious question of how such revenue should be used.

The corrective nature of pollution charges provides a 'double dividend': a revenue-neutral tax policy change, combining the introduction of pollution charges with the reduction or elimination of other taxes, would both protect the environment by reducing harmful emissions and offset market distortions associated with other taxes (for example, US personal and corporate income taxes generate distortions or pure losses of 20 to 50 cents for each dollar collected). This double dividend may be particularly relevant in today's political climate where policy makers are reluctant to consider any new taxes."

and, more recently:

"... a carbon tax (in 2050) of \$150 to \$200 per ton of carbon reduces the probability of dangerous anthropogenic interference from about 45% without policy change to controls to nearly zero."[8]

Even these prescient ideas did not provide for an 'energy dividend' as discussed in Chapter 7.

Cabinet Memo

(Cabinet Memo's are key to operation of the British-style civil service. A Cabinet Memo should be no longer than four pages, and cover:

Background,

The Problem,

Alternatives, (with advantages and disadvantages) and

Recommendation.

It being the considered opinion of the civil service that if a problem cannot be described and solved within four pages, it is not properly understood.

In real life, a Cabinet Memo is drafted by one department, ideally by Environment but in practice by Treasury as "Senior Department". It is then critiqued and reworded by all other interested departments, until a unified document is agreed upon. Here is Global Warming in four pages.)

Arresting Global Warming

<u>Background</u>: There is now a well established scientific consensus that human use of fossil fuels (coal, oil, natural gas, limestone, tar sands and potentially methane clathrates) is leading to increased concentrations of atmospheric carbon dioxide (ACO2), which in turn is leading to "global warming", loss of sea-ice, melting glaciers, melting permafrost, rising sea levels, extreme and damaging weather, forest fires, floods and droughts. ACO2 levels are already above anything experienced in the last 450,000 years.

A number of computer "climate models" have been shown to track well against historic data. How well they will predict the future is unknown, since there are no records to test them against for the levels of ACO2 being induced. Melting of sea ice and glaciers provides one "positive feedback" that has been tested; reduced ice-cover results in increased energy absorption and temperature rise, leading to more melting. Other potential feed-back mechanisms that could lead to sudden increases in ACO2, and rapid and unpredictable temperature and sea level rise, exist such as burning of tropical and northern forests, melting of the permafrost, loss of the Greenland or Antarctic glaciers, or the release of methane stored as clathrate on the polar sea floor. The tundra alone contains enough carbon to double ACO2. Thus there is a danger of unpredictable and irreversible increases in ACO2, possibly leading to an unstoppable sea-level rise of 20 to 200 feet.

Developed countries (especially the U.S.) have contributed most to the inventory of ACO2, however developing country emissions are rising rapidly, China surpassed the U.S. as the economy with highest annual ACO2 releases in 2006.

Recent research has shown that it is technically feasible to collect CO_2 from the atmosphere and concentrate it suitable for sequestration in exhausted oil fields, other suitable geological structures, or to be converted to magnesium or calcium carbonate. Unfortunately some technical and cost problems remain to be solved before it can be used in a major CO_2 sequestration program.

There is very little recognition amongst the general public, industry leaders (or indeed the political leadership) of the urgent need to dispense with fossil energy.

The Problem: The problem is three fold:

i)   How to reduce (and eventually eliminate) our fossil CO_2 emissions at least cost,

ii) How to induce other countries to join with us in eliminating fossil CO_2 emissions, and

iii) A widespread belief that "business as usual" is a viable option.

Alternatives:

i) *Do Nothing.* This is always an alternative, but in this case is almost certainly a non-starter, since it implies a 200 foot sea level rise (drowning all major coastal cities) in from 90 to 270 years.

ii) *Technology Development and Energy Efficiency.*

Advantages: California has had substantial success in encouraging utilities to show consumers how to save electricity (per household usage is only 7,000 kWh, versus 13,000 for the U.S. as a whole). Relatively modest increases in efficiency in wind farms, solar thermal and plug-in hybrids would likely make them cost competitive with fossil energy. If collecting CO_2 from the atmosphere becomes economic, this would lay the foundation for actually reducing the level of ACO_2.

Disadvantage: Fails to mobilize market forces to reinforce a switch to renewable energy.

iii) *Cap and Trade.*

Advantages: Sets definite upper limit on fossil fuel use, and "puts a price on pollution", thus mobilizing market forces to help switch to fossil free energy sources.

Would be popular with polluters who would get windfall profits. Major source of political contributions from polluters wishing to preserve their caps.

Disadvantages: As generally proposed caps would be allocated to industries on the basis of historic levels of CO_2 emissions. This "rewards established polluters" and gives them a free-ride up to the level of their cap. Monitoring of a large number of decentralized sites is likely to be difficult. As carbon credits are traded, purchasers are likely to pass the cost onto consumers, with a dead-weight loss for consumers and windfall profits for polluters. If caps are set too low, they might lead to power cuts. Major source of political corruption, see "Advantages" above.

iv) *Revenue Neutral, Carbon Tax.* (A tax of $250 ton of carbon would allow payroll taxes to be cut by a third)

Advantages: Could be collected at the mine, well-head or when imported, thus simplifying monitoring. Tax revenue would come to the government, to be used to lower or eliminate other taxes (that is the revenue neutral provision). Mobilizes market forces to help switch to fossil free energy. Should be no government induced black-outs. Could explain to consumers that higher energy costs were being balanced by removal of other taxes, such as payroll tax. Tax rate could be adjusted in the light of experience.

Disadvantages: Would be unpopular with polluters, since they would not get windfall profit. Hard to hit a quantitative target for fossil fuel use, since the policy would set the tax rate, not the quantity of fossil fuel to be used. Voters allergic to *any* tax increase. Offsetting reduction in payroll taxes would provide no offsetting benefits to those (retirees, unemployed, etc.) who do not pay the tax.

v) *Carbon Tax with Energy Dividend.* (A tax of $250 of carbon would provide a dividend of about $166 per month, per registered voter.)

Advantages: As for (iv) above, plus would be benefit all eligible citizens/voters, thus excluding green-card holders and illegal immigrants. Would mobilize voter as well as market forces for the switch to fossil-free energy, and immunize the majority of voters against usual opposition to tax increases, would encourage voter registration: The key to participatory democracy. Would provide votes to counter the likely large financial contributions from polluters designed to protect themselves.

<u>Disadvantages</u>: Industry opposition, as above.

vi) *Ban on New Fossil Fuelled Power Plants.*

<u>Advantages</u>: Would signal how very seriously the Government takes the problem of global warming, and its political commitment to strong and effective action, would finally force industry and consumers to face the need for new answers and life styles, would be politically popular as showing the Government "is finally doing something".

<u>Disadvantages</u>: Would be highly politically unpopular as consumers lost access to cheap energy, and would generate strong opposition from the fossil fuel interests.

vii) *Host an Annual International Consultation.*

<u>Advantages</u>: This would bring together the leading three or four people most responsible for reducing ACO2 emissions in each country, for a week of reports and presentations on what is working, what progress has been made, and mutual reinforcement. This would be a technical, informal international consultation amongst the technicians most directly involved. It would avoid the political maneuvering characteristic of formal international agreements.

<u>Disadvantages</u>: Cost, perhaps $10 million a year.

<u>Recommendation</u>:

It is recommended that the government adopt alternatives (ii), (v), (vi) and (vii): *Technology Development and Energy Efficiency, Carbon Tax with Energy Dividend* ($250 ton of carbon, and dividend of $166 per voter per month), *Ban on New Fossil Power Plants* and *Host an Annual International Consultation.* These four policies should be pursued simultaneously.

Chapter 1:   The Carbon Cycle

Conceptually simple, the carbon cycle is nevertheless miss-understood or ignored by many in discussing what can be done about global warming. If you can already explain why it makes no sense to talk of offsetting the burning of coal by planting trees, there may be little new you will gain from this chapter. However, if trees for coal looks like a sensible offset, read on.

At its simplest, the carbon cycle involves atmospheric carbon dioxide being converted to plant material (biomass, mostly lignocellulosic biomass) by photosynthesis, and then the plant material being converted to atmospheric carbon dioxide by burning, decay or consumption by animals. Schematically this can be represented as in Figure 1.

Atmosphere: CO2 + H2O + sunlight

                                                    V

                                          Photosynthesis

                                                    V

Sequestered: Biomass   + O2

                                                    V

                                Burning, decay and animals

                                                    V

Atmosphere: CO2 + H2O + energy

Figure 1: The Core of the Carbon Cycle

Think about it for a moment, we either learnt Figure 1 at high school, or know it from common sense. The basic relationships are:

i)   Plants take atmospheric carbon dioxide (CO2) and water (H2O) (from the root zone) and energy from the sun, and by the bio-chemical process known as photosynthesis convert them to plant material and oxygen(O2) that is released to the atmosphere.

ii) The plant material may sequester (store) the carbon for days, years or centuries.

iii) Eventually the plant material burns, decays or is eaten by animals. When this occurs oxygen is combined with the plant material to yield carbon dioxide, water and energy. In the case of fire, the energy is easily identified as the heat given off. But animals equally obtain their life-energy from the food they eat. As is well known, animals take in oxygen from the atmosphere and release water vapor and carbon dioxide, when they breath.

Within this core (and over-simplified) carbon cycle, the total carbon involved is fixed, it is present either as atmospheric carbon dioxide (ACO2), biomass, animals or organisms. This does not mean the amount of ACO2 is fixed, since the amount of carbon stored in the biomass can change. If the CO2 is photosynthesized into an annual plant, it is likely to decay (or be eaten) within a year, and thus returned to ACO2. If the CO2 is photosynthesized into a tree it may be centuries before it is returned to ACO2 by decay or forest fire.

The general trend for the last thousand years or so has been for people to replace forests with agriculture, thus adding ACO2 as trees have been burned or destroyed to be replaced by annual crops. This has not changed the amount of CO2 in the carbon cycle, but has increased the proportion of carbon in the cycle held as ACO2.

There are three other major contributors/players in the natural carbon cycle:

i) Volcanoes can emit huge amounts of CO2 and methane that is transformed into CO2 within months, to the atmosphere thus *adding* to the carbon in the cycle[9].

ii) Oceans can absorb (and release) CO2. Higher concentrations of ACO2 leads to the ocean to absorbing CO2, thus becoming less alkaline[10]. While lower concentrations of ACO2 can

2

lead the ocean to release CO_2. Currently it is estimated that the ocean absorbs about 40% of fossil-carbon added to the atmosphere. Other things equal (especially ACO_2 concentration) oceans hold less CO_2 as they get warmer.

iii) When plant material decays in the absence of oxygen, as in bogs or marshes (or in animals guts) methane rather than CO_2 may be produced. Methane is a much more effective greenhouse gas, however it is relatively short lived usually being converted to CO_2 within about three months.

Refinements to the Carbon Cycle: Methane is a part of the carbon cycle. Animals and anaerobic decay can produce methane (CH_4) rather than CO_2. Methane has a warming potential of 23 (23 times as effective as carbon dioxide in blocking heat loss)[11] but combines with oxygen within months to form CO_2 and water. Most decay, most animal digestion and all burning produces CO_2 directly, but methane is an inherent part of the carbon cycle.

Atmosphere: CO_2 + H_2O + sunlight
                                       V
                                 Photosynthesis
                                       V
Sequestered: Biomass + O_2
                                       V
                         Burning, decay and animals
                             | | V
                             | | CH_4 + 2 O_2 + energy
                         V   V   V
Atmosphere: CO_2 + H_2O + energy

Figure 2: Methane in the Carbon Cycle

Outside the Limits: That is about it, for the natural carbon cycle. Figure 3 shows the long-term relationship between ACO_2 and temperature, taken from ice-cores. This record goes back to about

450,000 years ago. Clearly CO2 level and temperature are correlated (move together) in Figure 3. This does not tell us if temperature rise causes CO2 rise or vica versa. It appears that historically temperature has been the driving force. As temperature rose, for whatever reason, it led to increased releases of CO2 (from forest fires, melting tundra and methane hydrates perhaps), that helped cause further warming. Our experience (on the far right of the graph) is clearly the other way round, with increased levels of ACO2, leading to global warming and quite possibly further releases of ACO2. The fastest increase in ACO2 levels shown in the ice-core was a rise of 30 ppm over roughly a 1,000 year period. In the last *17* years we have seen a similar increase. Temperature is not yet higher than has been experienced a number of times in the past but ACO2 concentrations are way above anything experienced (and rising far faster than) at any time in the last 450,000 years[12].

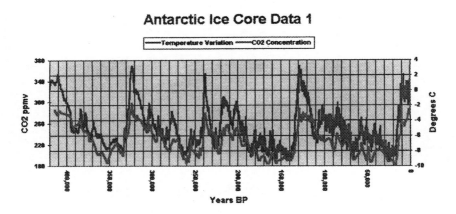

Figure 3. CO2 and Temperature Variations from Ice-Core Data[13]

Figure 4 gives estimated ACO2 concentrations from 1750 to the present day. The black line is carbon dioxide concentration in ppm (parts per million) and the grey line is predicted emissions. From 1958 the ACO2 is from actual measurements at Mona Loa Observatory, Hawaii, earlier ACO2 levels are based on ice-core data. As shown in Figure 5, there is a swing of about 6 ppm (parts per million) during any given year, caused by the northern hemisphere spring and summer when plant growth withdraws CO2 from the atmosphere only to be followed by an upswing in the northern autumn and winter, as plant material decays. This annual swing is around a clearly rising and accelerating trend. ACO2 levels have risen at Mauna Loa from about 315 ppm in 1960 to 380 ppm in 2006.

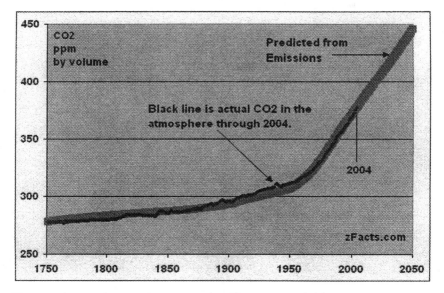

Figure 4: Atmospheric Carbon Dioxide (ACO2) 1750 to 2050[14].

Table 1: Cumulative Emissions to 2005[15]

Country	Contribution (%)
U.S.A.	27.8
China	7.8
Russia	7.5
Germany	6.7
U.K.	6.1
Japan	3.9
India	2.4
Rest of Europe	18.3
Rest of World	12.5
Ships/Air	4.0
Other	3.0

As shown in Table 1, developed countries are responsible for about 75 percent of the increase in ACO2 since 1850. This said, China is thought to have overtaken the U.S. in 2006, as the country with highest rate of AFCO2TA[16].

The Mona Loa data are shown in more detail in Figure 5:

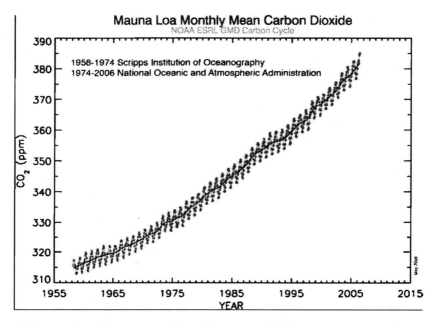

Figure 5: Concentration of Atmospheric CO2, recorded at Mona Loa, Hawaii[17].

Sleeping Dogs: Within the carbon cycle there are three giant reserves of sequestered CO2. These are:

Forests that take decades or centuries to reach maturity, during which time they absorb more carbon than they give off, thus representing at maturity a major store of bio-carbon that has been withdrawn from the atmosphere. Natural decay and growth for a mature forest withdraws as much ACO2 as it releases. However, if a forest burns it can return bio-carbon stored over centuries to the atmosphere in a matter of days. Global temperature and associated climate changes can affect the likelihood of forests fires. Should we induce further major forest fires in the Amazon, Congo, Indonesia or northern arboreal forests, this could result in a major release ("burp") in bio-carbon, from within the carbon cycle producing a measurable increase in ACO2. We know that such a vicious feed-back loop is possible, we do not know what level of ACO2 would be necessary to trigger such all encompassing forest fires. The Amazon alone is reported as having the potential to add 10% to man-made emissions a year for seventy-five years (or to double man-made emissions for seven and a half years)[18]. We have some idea as to how such a catastrophe could occur:

"The problem is that (in the Amazon) the trees in some parts of the forest are responsible for as much as 74 per cent of local rainfall. As they start to die when temperature rises, less water is released into the air by the forest. This has three effects: there is less rainfall to sustain the remaining trees, more sunlight reaches the forest floor (drying it and making the forest more susceptible to fires), and less heat is lost through evaporation. The rising temperature and decreasing rainfall kill more trees, and the chain reaction continues. It could happen swiftly: 'we suggest' the researchers say, 'that this threshold exists very near to current climatic conditions'"[19].

Clearly, if our AFC2OTA were to trigger such a massive shift of bio-carbon from sequestered to atmospheric, all bets as to time for temperatures to rise, ice to melt, and oceans to rise, would be off. Truly we live in dangerous times.

The Siberian and Canadian *tundra* and permafrost represent another huge reserve of sequestered biomass. This is clearly bio-mass for which the carbon has been withdrawn from the atmosphere by photosynthesis, but over a very long time period. At current temperatures, the permafrost represents a withdrawal of carbon from the carbon cycle, stored/sequestered over thousands of year. If it is classified as being "within the carbon cycle" it would be catastrophic to have it returned as ACO2 to the cycle. Absent global warming, permafrost accumulates by being frozen solid over winter. In summer a few inches of the surface melts, and plant growth occurs only to be frozen (without decay) the following winter. Slowly this growth and freeze cycle accumulates frozen plant material. As global warming proceeds we can expect that some of the erstwhile permafrost will be unfrozen long enough to decay (thus adding ACO2), and also exposing new layers of permafrost to melt and decay. Again we know that this process has started in parts of the north, but do no know how much further warming would be needed to trigger widespread releases. A West Siberian bog alone is believed to contain 70 billion tons of methane, whose liberation would equate to 73 years of current manmade AFCO2TA[20]. Another source estimates that the total Artic permafrost contains 1,000 billion tons of carbon, enough if all released to double the current ACO2[21].

The third huge reserve of sequestered carbon is in the form of solid *methane hydrate* (also known as methane clathrate). It is not clear whether this methane hydrate was ever part of the carbon cycle, or how it got sequestered on the ocean floor. It is similar to fossil carbon, in having been out of the carbon cycle for millions of year, but unlike the other fossil carbons, it could under the right circumstance volatilize to atmospheric methane and then ACO2. (Fortunately we do not have to worry about wild-coal fires, which would be an analogous phenomenon.) This solid form of methane exists in waters more than 1,300 feet deep and at temperatures below 1 degree centigrade (34-35 degrees Fahrenheit). The methane is kept in solid form by the pressure of the overlying water. In total methane hydrate is ten times as plentiful as natural gas, with perhaps twice the energy of all other fossil fuels combined. Fortunately most of it is locked away at a great depth. Tim Flannery warns:

"If pressure on the clathrates were ever relieved, or the temperature of the deep oceans were to increase, colossal amounts of methane could be released. We have seen the consequences of one such release in the North Sea 55 million years ago, but paleontologists are now beginning to suspect that the unleashing of the clathrates may have been responsible for a far more profound change--the biggest extinction of all time.

Two hundred and forty-five million years ago, around nine out of ten species living on earth became extinct. Known as the Permo-Triassic extinction event, it carried off an early radiation of mammal-like creatures….

So vast was this input of greenhouse gas to the atmosphere (from the impact of an asteroid, or massive volcanic eruptions) that it was thought to have led to an initial rise in global average temperature of about 11 degrees Fahrenheit (6 degrees Centigrade). .... Such was the total impact of increasing temperature thereby generated that it triggered the release of huge volumes of methane from the tundra and clathrates of the sea floor."[22]

Some clathrates are stored at relatively shallow depths in the polar seas.

Note that in each of these three cases (sometimes referred to as "tipping points") a rise in ACO2, by raising global temperatures, would trigger release of the sequestered material, resulting in a very substantial addition to ACO2. The danger is that as additional fossil CO2 is added to the atmosphere, at some point the balance between sequestered and ACO2, would shift significantly in favor of ACO2, with a sudden acceleration of increases in global warming, and climate change.

Another unknown is that the oceans cannot be relied upon to go on absorbing 40% of emissions. Should temperature and wind changes lead to greater depth segmentation of the ocean, especially a segmentation that would lead to a thinner surface layer that did not mix with lower layers, then the oceans capacity to absorb CO2 would be reduced. By the same token if greater mixing took place, absorption rates could be expected to increase.

A Matter of Time Scale: It should be emphasized that when plants burn, decay or are eaten, the resulting bio-CO2 is being *returned* to the atmosphere, as it was previously *withdrawn* by photosynthesis.

By contrast, when fossil fuels are burnt, the fossil-CO2 released is being *added* to the atmosphere, since it has either never been withdrawn through photosynthesis or was withdrawn *many millions* of year ago.

We distinguish bio- and fossil-carbon for expository purposes, depending on the source of the CO2. There is, however, no chemical test of ACO2 that would allow us to determine which molecules came from bio-carbon and which from fossil. Once fossil-CO2 is added to the atmosphere it mixes indistinguishably with the CO2 already there and may be used equally with bio-CO2 for photosynthesis, and is thus transformed itself into bio-CO2. In principle we could ask a molecule of CO2 for how many generations it had been in the biological cycle. We have, however, no chemical test that would tell us this.

Manipulating the Cycle. We have seen that not all carbon in the carbon cycle is present as ACO2, indeed ACO2 comprises less than 2 percent of the carbon in the cycle. Vegetation and soils comprise another 5 percent, with the balance in the oceans. To the extent that trees sequester carbon for decades or centuries, they can be very useful in reducing the ACO2 in the cycle. By the same token, the slow accumulation of permafrost on the tundra, has in the past made a small, but useful annual withdrawal of ACO2. Similarly the oceans are still absorbing CO2 from the atmosphere (equivalent to about 40% of annual fossil carbon additions each year).

When we use fossil fuels we affect the *amount* of carbon in the cycle, when we plant (or burn) trees or affect the permafrost, we affect the *location* of carbon within the cycle.

Unfortunately, as we AFCO2TA and raise the ACO2, this leads to warming, that tends to manipulate the cycle adversely (generates feed-back) so that forest fires are more likely and permafrost melts, thus leading to more of the carbon in the cycle being in the form of ACO2. We return to this topic in Chapter 4.

Energy Capture in the Cycle: When we use wood to light a fire, we are generating useful energy as we return carbon to the atmosphere, similarly animals generate their life-energy when the eat biomass and breath out CO2. In many other situations biological decay leads to the carbon in biomass being *returned* to the atmosphere without evident useful energy being generated. Interestingly, Indian farmers have used dried cow dung as cooking fuel for generations, thus capturing useful energy as the carbon is burned and returned to the atmosphere. Anaerobic decay of dung in farm lagoons or of biomass in land-fills generates methane, which can be burned to produce useful energy even as carbon is returned to the atmosphere.

Concentration of ACO2: We have records as to the amount of ACO2, that allow us to estimate the rate of addition of fossil-CO2, and hence the inventory/proportion of existing ACO2 that has been added since the widespread use of fossil fuels began (circa 1850)[23].

It has long been known that ACO2 could affect the Earth's temperature[24]. By 1910 Svante Arrhenius, a Swedish chemist, had demonstrated that the ice-ages could have been generated by changes in the level of ACO2. And, in 1938, in an address to the Royal Metrological Society, Guy Callandar, showed that the world was warming, and suggested that that the cause was industrial activity and the use of fossil fuels.

However, it was not until 1957 that the systematic collection of data on ACO2 concentrations commenced. The observations were made at the Mauna Loa Observatory in Hawaii. The result is the remarkably consistent saw-toothed curve show in Figure 5.

Sequestration (or storage): In addition to the natural stores of carbon within the carbon cycle, discussed above, there is interest in storing (sequestering) carbon as CO_2. One possibility is to capture CO_2 from the flue gasses of power stations. This is discussed further in Chapter 5. Recent work by Prof. Klaus Lackner of Columbia University has demonstrated the possibility of capturing CO_2 directly from the atmosphere. Even though the concentration of CO_2 is "only" 380 ppm (or 0.04%), yet by passing enough air over sodium hydroxide a substantial volume of CO_2 can be collected. It is necessary to then get the sodium hydroxide to give up its CO_2, so that it can start collecting CO_2 from the atmosphere again. Just as we have wind-farms, we may one day be able to have wind-"sponges" or arrays of sodium hydroxide CO_2 collectors in windy places. Current estimates of cost of atmospheric capture and storage is about $400 per ton of carbon[25]. There is hope that this cost can be cut to a third, at which stage it might become economic.

Once captured, CO_2 can be stored in exhausted oil or gas fields, and some geological formations. It is essential that such geological formations be tightly sealed. Since CO_2 is 50% heavier than air, a significant escape would likely flow to the lowest point and pool, thus driving out oxygen and suffocating people and animals, as occurred due to a natural eruption of CO2 in Lake Nyos in Cameroon in August 1986. It can also be stored as CO2 clathrates in the deep ocean. This development opens the possibility of eventually being able to control ACO2 levels.

Units: Discussion of global warming is bedeviled by a variety of different units, often with the same (or nearly the same) name. Thus temperature may be in Fahrenheit or Centigrade, and "tons of" can refer to carbon or carbon dioxide, or even "carbon dioxide equivalent (CO2e)" when discussing the concentration of greenhouse gasses.

Scientists work with Centigrade. 5 degrees Centigrade corresponds to 9 degrees Fahrenheit, or *roughly* 2 degrees Fahrenheit per degree Centigrade. We will go along with the scientist and refer to *degrees centigrade* for the most part.

Absolute temperatures are not much used in the global warming literature rather the focus is in departures from historical norms. For what it is worth, we can note that water freezes at 0 degrees Centigrade or 32 degrees Fahrenheit.

Another thing to watch out for, is that it is generally agreed that from pre-industrial times (circa 1850) temperature has risen by 0.6 degrees Centigrade. Thus in interpreting temperature change projections it is important to note whether the change is from pre-industrial times, or from "today" (circa 2007). When an author claims that we could adjust to a temperature rise of 2 degrees, it makes a big difference if he is measuring the change from pre-industrial times, (in which case he is asserting that we could adjust to a *further* rise of 1.4 degrees Centigrade) or the present day (i.e. a *total* increase of 2.6 degrees Centigrade from pre-industrial times).

Reference will be made primarily to tons of carbon (tons of carbon dioxide = 3.67x(tons of carbon)), and occasionally to CO2 equivalent (CO2e). CO2e is the amount of CO2 with the global heating effect of all greenhouse gasses (including CO2).

   <u>Magnitudes</u>: Approximately 6.3 billion tons of carbon is emitted annually from the burning of fossil fuels and other industrial activities, and 1.7 billion tons from deforestation, for a total of 8.0 billion tons of carbon. Of this, 3.2 billion tons remain in the atmosphere and 2 billion tons are absorbed by the oceans, the balance, 2.8 billion tons are absorbed terrestrially mostly in northern forests, but also in soil and forests generally[26].

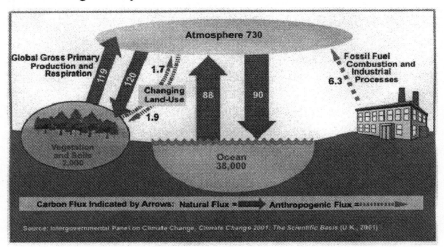

Figure 6: Global Carbon Cycle (Billion Metric Tons Carbon)[27]

   As shown in Figure 6, the IPPC's 2001 report, gave total carbon in the carbon cycle as:

	Billion m. Tons	%
Atmospheric CO2	730	1.79
Vegetation and Soil	2,000	4.91
Ocean	38,000	93.30
Total	40,730	100.00

Note the very small percentage of bio-carbon dioxide that is in the atmosphere. Only a small aberration in the amount of carbon held in the balance of the cycle, would lead to drastic changes in ACO2, with drastic changes in global temperatures and weather. As we ship trainloads of coal to our power stations to be added to ACO2, we are dealing with a very delicate system: No wonder measurable effects are being detected.

Annual changes were given as:

	Billion m. Tons
Addition to Atmosphere	
Fossil Fuels	6.3
Farming and Forestry	1.7
From Vegetation and Soil	119
From Oceans	88
Total	215
Subtractions from Atmosphere	
By Farming and Forestry	1.9
By Vegetation and Soil	120
By Oceans	90
Total	211.9
Net Addition	3.1

"Farming and Forestry" refers to changes in land use. Petrol and fertilizers used in farming and forestry are reported under fossil fuels.

The net result from Figure 6, is that of the 6.3 billion metric tons of carbon released by the use of fossil fuels, 3.2 billion tons are sequestered or stored, mostly in the ocean, and 3.1 billion tons remain in the atmosphere leading to the steady increase in ACO_2 concentrations.

A billion tons of carbon is also referred to as a giga ton of carbon (GtC) 280 ppm (approximate atmospheric concentration in 1750-1850) of CO_2 equates to 596.4 GtC. 380 ppm of CO_2 (the current concentration of CO_2) amounts to 809.4 GtC. An addition of 3 GtC in any one year would thus appear not to make much difference. The problem is addition of 3 GtC year after year, *and the amount that has already been released.*

Major Polluters: China and the United States are the leading polluters, China having passed the United States in 2006 by releasing 6.2 billion m. tons of CO2 (1.68 billion m. tons of carbon), versus 5.8 billion m.tons of CO2 (1.58 billion m. tons of carbon) by the United States[28]. As discussed above the 2001 IPCC report said that 6.3 billion tons of carbon were released from fossil fuels, and 1.7 billion from farming and forestry, for a total world release from these two sources of 8 billion m. tons of carbon. Global release data for 2006 is not available. If total releases have risen to (the conveniently round number of) 10 billion m. tons[29] then China would be contributing 16.8 percent of global emissions, and the U.S. 15.8 percent. Thus if the U.S. achieved zero emissions, this would reduce global emissions by about 16 percent, a very significant number.

Exactly because they are such major polluters, China and the US have it in their power, acting alone, to go a long way towards arresting global warming. With global net annual additions of 3.1 billion m. tones of carbon, the US and China have total gross contributions 3.26 billion m. tons, nominally enough to reduce net emissions to zero. However, the carbon cycle is quite complex and lower emissions would likely lead to lower oceanic sequestration, and in any case immediate cessation of use of all fossil fuels would involve too great economic disruption. Nevertheless *it is clear that what these two countries do (or fail to do) matters greatly,* in contrast to say Estonia, where the global impact of lowered emissions would be imperceptible, albeit important.

Need to Know: Ideally a climate projection should be able to tell us for a given year:

i)The rate of adding carbon dioxide to the atmosphere,

ii) The absolute concentration (ppm) of ACO2,

iii) The current global temperature, relative to a baseline,

iv) The eventual equilibrium temperature, on the assumption that no further fossil-carbon was added to the atmosphere, and

v) How long it will take to reach this equilibrium.

Some of these figures may be available only as a range. However, it is important to distinguish between current temperature and equilibrium temperature; and between current rate of emissions, and the cumulative emission to date.

The U.S. Department of Energy is proceeding on the assumption that: *Fossil fuels will remain the mainstay of energy production well into the 21st century*[30]. It would be salutary if they also had to add "by which time it is expected that ACO2 will be in the neighborhood of 1000 ppm"; and indeed "global temperatures will have risen by 7 degrees Centigrade, and sea levels are expected to be 20 feet higher", or some such. Adding these other dimensions to the DOE assumptions, would clearly reveal the costs of continuing to rely on coal and prompt the question: *At what ppm does the DOE expect to dispense with coal?*

Chapter 2: Global Warming: An Economic Problem

Research largely determines the future technological choices that we will have. But *prices* determine *which of our currently available technologies will be used*, and indeed which technical possibilities venture capitalists will commercialize.

Politicians and other leaders are inclined to focus on the technical problems of reducing (fossil) energy use, thus they announce multi-billion dollar research programs to develop fuel cells or bring forward "the hydrogen economy", designed to yield results in a decade or so. What is needed, of course, is *to persuade people to make better choices amongst the various technologies available today.* With a much higher fossil-electricity price, demand would switch to fossil-free electricity. In the first instance this would force up the price of fossil-free electricity too, that would in turn jump-start venture capitalists interest in developing new sources of fossil-free electricity; and persuading electric power generating companies to switch from fossil to nuclear power plants, wind and solar. These are supply side effects. In the face of higher prices lights and appliances would be turned off when not needed, thermostats would be adjusted and fossil-electricity consumption reduced in a thousand ways: There would be important demand side effects.

Higher gasoline prices would persuade people to car pool, use public transport and above all else trade in their SUV's for smaller cars (especially hybrids) with better mileage. Higher air fares would lead to fewer flights, as people decided to vacation closer to home, to visit relatives less frequently or organize a video conference in place of a physical meeting. The would be important demand side effects[31]. *The ways we could adjust our lives with present technology is almost limitless*, but when energy is cheap, why change?

There is, of course, the regulatory approach to try to achieve the same outcome. Electricity and gas could be rationed: "only x units per month". The problem with the regulatory (or "central planning") approach is that it is highly cumbersome, and individual needs vary dramatically. As a retiree I need to keep my home heated all day, but scarcely need my car. Five years ago I needed to heat my home for five hours a day (otherwise I was in bed or at work), but needed to drive my car 80 miles a day, since I had no readily available public transport. The balance of electricity and gasoline that I need to consume has changed dramatically. It is very hard to design a regulatory/rationing system that will accommodate the diversity of actual needs. Price on the other hand leaves me free to choose the balance of (expensive) energy that I can afford to consume. (But see Chapter 8 for an interesting proposal to ration carbon to consumers directly).

Not only is global warming an economic problem, because price is the policy tool of choice but also because the key cause of global warming is "market failure" a well studied economic phenomena. *Market failure* occurs when consumers and producers get the wrong price signals. The problem in the case of global warming being that users of fossil fuels do not have to pay anything for releasing CO_2 and other greenhouse gasses.

The atmosphere "belongs" to everyone[32], or no one. We can all breath it at no expense, use its oxygen for fires, and release CO_2 without charge.

We now know that fossil fuels released over the last century and a half have massively elevated the levels of ACO2 (atmospheric carbon dioxide), with now discernable adverse environmental effects. From a global perspective the cost of already released fossil-CO2 will be enormous, but only by chance will there be any connection between the amount of fossil fuel used and the adverse consequences. It is clear that the major polluters have been the developed countries of the West (and former Soviet Union), while the first round of adverse effects seem likely to be a loss of rainfall in Africa and flooding particularly in Bangladesh and some small Pacific island nations[33]. Only in Australia do we appear to be seeing a rough equation of benefits and costs, its massive coal exports being perhaps balanced by a recent and protracted drought.

One of the worst features of the disconnect between polluters and those adversely affected, is that there is no emotional connection between (or consciousness of) the person (impersonally) causing the suffering, and those that suffer. We mean no harm, when we turn on the light, but it is becoming increasingly clear that we indeed do harm, perhaps in total much greater than the benefit from having a light[34]. Increasingly conscious of this connection, some people are beginning to modify their lifestyle to reduce their AFCO2TA. We return to this topic in the next chapter.

It was suggested above that, by chance, there may be an approximate equation of costs and benefits of global warming for Australia. Note, however, that market failure means that despite Australia doing about as much harm as it suffers, it cannot modify its behavior to avoid the harm. Suppose that Australia stopped all coal exports, what would happen? Firstly Indonesia or America would likely step in to make up the shortfall, with basically no affect on global warming. However, suppose further that no one stepped in to replace the Australian supply, and world AFCO2TA was reduced in line with lowered Australian exports. There would be a minor adjustment to the rate of AFCO2TA world-wide, and a probably imperceptible change in the intensity of the Australian drought.

In the case of global warming market failure is absolutely vicious since there is no incentive for an individual, *or a nation*, to reduce AFCO2TA: We have seen Australia and America stand aside from Kyoto.

If in the United States we are concerned at the pollution of the Chesapeake Bay, there are national environmental laws that can be relied on to support the effort. Furthermore the system of national laws encourages the states most directly involved with the Chesapeake to collaborate for mutual benefit. We can quickly corral all those causing and suffering from pollution. If the concerned communities and states are unable to reach agreement, then at some stage the pollution problem would come to the attention of the (national) Environmental Protection Agency (EPA). The EPA would propose regulations, and allow public discussion. When the regulations were promulgated, no one could opt out.

By contrast there are no international environmental laws, and no international agency with enforcement powers. The closest thing to an international environmental agency is the United Nations Environmental Program, but this is an educational, research and facilitating program, totally without enforcement powers. It is extremely hard to get all those nations causing and suffering from global warming (i.e. ALL nations) to negotiate mutually supportive actions to reduce global warming. Moreover, any such agreement is a "one shot effort" that has to be repeated almost *de novo* when more decisive action is called for. Clearly Montreal and Kyoto are better than nothing, but that is damning with faint praise.

Everyday, every report, brings new evidence that the human race will pay an enormous price for failing to develop a system of enforceable environmental laws that would prevent individual countries from ignoring the popular will. It is unconscionable that the United States and Australia were able to "stand aside" from the Kyoto accord. "The answer" provided by this book refers to a nation, state, province or city (with relevant legal authority) *that wishes to reduce AFCO2TA* at least cost or maximum benefit. Pending the development of a global decision making process, it is not clear what would be meant by a "global policy recommendation". In chapter eleven we make brief and unsatisfactory suggestions with respect to this intractable problem.

Before turning to a discussion of modeling (the primary way people try to assess what lies ahead) it is worth reiterating that this book is about *stopping* adding fossil carbon dioxide to the atmosphere. That is stopping the use of coal, natural gas, oil, oilsands and clearly there is going to be some economic disruption if we reduce the use of fossil fuels, but nothing like the disruption there will be if we continue

Box 1: Stern on Costs

The ambition of policy has an impact on estimates of costs.

A Common feature of the model projections was the presence of increasing marginal costs to mitigation. This applies not just to the total mitigation achieved, but also to the speed at which it is brought about. This means reduction of GHG (Greenhouse Gasses) becomes more expensive as abatement increases in ambition and speed. Chapter 13 discusses findings from model comparisons and shows non-linear acceleration of costs as more ambitious stabilization paths are pursued. The relative absence of energy model results for stabilization concentration below 500 ppm CO2e (CO2 equivalence of heating effect of all greenhouse gas emissions) is explained by the fact that carbon-energy models found very significant cost associated with moving below 450 ppm, as the number of affordable mitigation options was quickly exhausted. Some models were unable to converge on a solution at such low stabilization levels, reflecting the absence of mitigation options and inflexibilities in the diffusion of 'backstop' technologies.

In general, model comparisons find that the cost of stabilizing emissions at 500-550 ppm CO2e would be around a third of doing so at 450-500 ppm CO2e.

The lesson here is to avoid doing too much, too fast, and to pace the flow of mitigation appropriately. For example great uncertainty remains as to the costs of very deep reductions. Digging down to emission reductions of 60-80% or more relative to baseline will require progress in reducing emissions from industrial processes, aviation, and a number of areas where it is presently hard to envisage cost-effective approaches. Thus a great deal depends on assumptions about technological advance (see Chapters 9, 16 and 24). The ICMP (Innovation Comparison Modeling Project) studies of cost impacts to 2050 of aiming for around 500-550 ppm CO2e were below 1% of GDP for all but one model (IMACLIM) (acronym unknown), but they diverged afterwards. By 2100, some fell while others rose sharply, reflecting the greater uncertainty about the costs of seeking out successive new mitigation sources[35].

to use them. The only reason that we refrain from recommending the immediate cessation of their use, is the enormous economic disruption that this would cause.

The Stern Review (Box 1) provides a good example of the consensus lack of urgency, emerging from most discussions of model results. Several comments come to mind:

i) To minimize economic dislocation it is essential that the major direction of economic/climate policy be known, namely: *Policies will be introduced successively with the objective of eliminating the use of fossil fuels*. This much more than announcing a ppm stabilization objective, will guide investment and minimize the miss-allocation of capital. We are frequently told that "business hates uncertainty", that being the case we should be crystal clear that we intend to put Peabody Coal (and other coal companies) out of business: We are not talking "clean coal" but "no coal". Certainly, no coal without safe sequestration, which will likely make even free coal unprofitable.

ii) It is implicit in the view of the Stern Report, that stabilization at 500-550 ppm is just as acceptable as stabilization at 450-500 ppm. No basis for this judgment is provided. The only hint we have as to the difference between 450 and 500 ppm is "model results". But models (see next section) are just a codification of our current understanding of physical laws and their interactions. *We may be wrong*. Most models make no allowance for "burps" as long sequestered bio-carbon is returned to the atmosphere, for the very good reason that we do not know what would trigger such events. We can infer, however, that burps are less likely at 450 ppm than 550 ppm. We simply do not know what extra risks we are taking on by allowing stabilization at higher levels. If burps are involved then the real choice may be between 450 and, say 800 ppm. Moreover, if we take the Stern logic of ignoring risk, it would be even cheaper to stabilize at 750 ppm, 1000 ppm, you name it!

iii) "The lesson here is to avoid doing too much, too fast". No, the lesson is: *What ever we are going to do, start today.* The longer we delay, the faster we will have to apply our remedy: That is why the wasted years of the Clinton and Bush administrations are such a tragedy.

iv) We do not need to have a complete strategy defined. We can take a heuristic approach: Starting with one level of taxes or caps, knowing that this will move us in the right direction. A year later we will have a better fix on the economic dislocation caused, and reduction in fossil carbon use achieved, leading to a revised policy, still with the announced objective of eliminating the use of fossil fuels.

v) "Digging down to emission reductions of 60-80% or more relative to baseline will require progress in reducing emissions from industrial processes, aviation, and a number of areas where it is presently hard to envisage cost-effective approaches." Implicit in this statement is the view that "we do not have to change". *If we cannot find a cost-effective approach we will just have to do without.* Faced with this alternative cost-effective approaches will quickly be found. In the case of aviation, high speed trains could work wonders for trips under 1,000 miles. Much air travel (especially holiday travel) is discretionary, and faced with really high costs companies would be able, in many cases, to substitute video-conferencing.

vi) The Stern Review is ambiguous as to the connection between concentration of CO2, and CO2e. On page 5 the Review defines CO2e as "In total, the warming effect due to all (Kyoto) greenhouse gases emitted by human activities is now equivalent to around 430 ppm of carbon dioxide (hereafter, CO2 equivalent of CO2e)". On page 12 it says "if greenhouse gas concentrations were stabilized at today's level of 430 ppm CO2e", thus equating 380 ppm CO2 with 430 ppm CO2e, or saying that CO2 contributes 88 percent of the heating in CO2e. But on page 221 it says "The current concentration of carbon dioxide in the atmosphere accounts for around 70% of the total warming effect ('the redactive forcing') of all Kyoto Greenhouse gases", citing IPPC(2001). The DOE Energy Information Agency reports that in 2005, the U.S. emitted 7,147.2 million metric tons of CO2e, of which 6,008.6 million metric tons was CO2, indicating that in 2005, for the U.S. CO2 was 84.1% of CO2e emissions[36]. This tends to support the higher Stern Review figure. We will use conversion CO2 = 0.88 x CO2e.

Modeling: A climate "model" is a series of equations representing temperature, humidity, water vapor, wind velocity, ACO2, sunlight, barometric pressure, plant growth, oceanic sequestration and the like, that conform to the known laws of physics. The world's atmosphere is then represented by a series of three dimensional "boxes", stacked one on top of another, and side by side, so that any point in the world's atmosphere belongs to one box or another. The equations are then applied to a central point in each "box" (which is taken as representative of the whole "box") to reflect the impact of surrounding "boxes".

In most models the ocean is represented as a set of corresponding "squares" (or "one box deep" if you like), although models with at least two ocean "levels" are now becoming available.

The whole system (set of "boxes", well actually "representative points") has to be initialized as representative of a point in time. A standard time interval is then chosen, say an hour or half day, and the model (or equation system) then updates each representative point by how much it would have changed, given the status of surrounding points, over the given time interval. Clearly this is a very repetitive system, firstly each point has to be corrected for the impact of its adjacent points, and then the whole system has to be "stepped forward" for however many time intervals it takes to reach the time projection of interest. If the model is charged with projecting conditions in 2020 or 2050 on the basis of even daily increments that is a lot of computing.

Currently, these climate models (of which there are about a dozen) are used in two primary ways. The first is to ask: What would be the *final equilibrium* if we, say, doubled the concentration of ACO2? This is because the impact of increased ACO2 is by no means instantaneous. An initial injection of CO2, can result in warmer temperatures, that set off responses, such as melting of glaciers or permafrost, that in turn affect future temperatures, and sequestering of CO2 in the ocean or forests that affect the amount of ACO2. It is not until these various feed-back loops and sequestering have worked themselves out that the system can be expected to stabilize in a new equilibrium. Climate scientists often use a target of limiting total emissions so that ACO2 concentrations will be no more than double the level in 1850 (before the widespread use of fossil fuels). There is no benefit/cost or optimization analysis for stabilizing at this level, rather it is a convenient figure.

The Stern Review, has summarized estimates of the temperature rise associated with a range of final equilibrium (stabilization) levels of atmospheric CO2 equivalent (CO2e). CO2e being the CO2 level equivalent to the actual warming capacity of all greenhouse gasses. The results are shown in Table 2.

Current levels of ACO2e are 430 ppm[38], and current temperature is 0.6 degrees centigrade above its pre-industrial level. Making these two corrections yields Table 3, which expresses the change in ACO2e from today's level for stabilization, and associated estimates of temperature change from today's temperature, in degrees Fahrenheit.

Table 2: Temperature Increases at Equilibrium Relative to the Pre-Industrial Level (in degrees Centigrade)[37]

Stabilization Level ppm		←----------------Model*------------→		
CO2e	CO2	IPCC	Hadley	All Eleven
400	352	0.8 to 2.4	1.3 to 2.8	0.6 to 4.9
450	396	1.0 to 3.1	1.7 to 3.7	0.8 to 6.4
500	440	1.3 to 3.8	2.0 to 4.5	1.0 to 7.9
550	484	1.5 to 4.4	2.4 to 5.3	1.2 to 9.1
650	572	1.8 to 5.5	2.9 to 6.6	1.5 to 11.4
750	660	2.2 to 6.4	3.4 to 7.7	1.7 to 13.3
1000	880	2.8 to 8.3	4.4 to 9.9	2.2 to 17.1

* IPCC = Results reported in the IPCC's Third Assessment Report, 2001,
Hadley = Model from U.K. Hadley Research Center
All Eleven = All eleven models reviewed by the Stern Report.

Table 3: Temperature Increases at Equilibrium Relative to the Current Level (in degrees Fahrenheit)

Stabilization Change ppm		←----------------Model------------→		
CO2e	CO2	IPCC	Hadley	All Eleven
-30	-28	0.4 to 3.2	1.3 to 4.0	0.0 to 7.7
20	16	0.7 to 4.5	2.0 to 5.6	0.4 to 10.4
70	60	1.3 to 5.7	2.5 to 7.0	0.7 to 13.1
120	104	1.1 to 6.8	3.2 to 8.5	1.1 to 15.3
220	192	2.2 to 8.8	4.1 to 10.8	1.6 to 19.4
320	280	1.9 to 7.0	5.0 to 12.8	2.0 to 22.9
570	500	4.0 to 13.9	6.8 to 16.7	2.9 to 29.7

Table 4: Recent Annual Mean Growth Rate of CO2

Year	Change In ppm	Year	Change in ppm[39]
1971	0.78	2001	1.61
1972	1.79	2002	2.55
1973	1.18	2003	2.31
1974	0.76	2004	1.54
1975	1.09	2005	2.54
1976	0.90	2006	1.72

Table 4 gives the growth in annual mean CO2 concentrations at Moana Loa.

Think about Tables 3 and 4 for a moment. Table 3 says that even if we had been able to stabilize ACO2 at 28 ppm *less* than at present, (i.e at 352 ppm rather than 380 ppm) *we would still face a further increase in temperature* (from 0 to 7.7 oF) above today's mean temperature, as the 352 ppm of CO2 already in the atmosphere worked its way through various feed-back loops to reach equilibrium.

The higher rates of increase in ACO2 revealed in Table 4, reflect the very rapid (and coal dependent) industrialization going on India and China, together with continued relatively slow growth in the developed world, but with no perceptible movement away from fossil dependence.

If we managed to stabilize at 16 ppm above today's ACO2 concentration (or 396 ppm) we would face a temperature rise of from 0.7 to 10.4 oF. We are currently adding about 2 to 3 ppm of ACO2 per year, say 2.5 ppm. Within *six and a half years* this will add 16 ppm. We are not talking decades, we are talking years. "Stabilization" means no more AFCO2TA. No petrol driven cars, no air travel, no natural gas, and no fossil-generated electricity. No obviously, we are not going to stabilize to this extent within seven years, but the models are telling us *that means we are going to increase global temperatures significantly, quite possibly beyond crucial tipping points*: Global warming is an *urgent problem*. The current policy vacuum, verges on the criminal.

The key point is that far from our having decades to make difficult decisions, *we should have made them decades ago*. We need to decide that we are going to move as expeditiously as possible to a fossil-free future. We should not be afraid of "making the wrong decisions", decisions can be fine tuned as we learn, and if necessary reversed. However, as discussed in Chapters 7 (The Answer) and 12 (Action Program) the needed directions of policy change are pretty obvious. We need the decision on a fossil free future, and the first portfolio of supportive policies right now.

As discussed in the final chapter "Keeping Tabs", Table 4 can be refined to give monthly ACO2 levels. Projection of these monthly provides a poor-man's way to monitor actual progress, month by month. Ideally ACO2 concentrations this month should be *the same as* this month, last year. When this is achieved we will have stabilized ACO2 concentrations. How many billion people the resulting climate will support remains to be seen.

The second way in which these climate models are used, is to project the time path of adjustment to higher levels of ACO2. In these models, additional fossil-CO2 is injected into the system while the system is still adjusting to previous injections, this might be termed a "disequilibrium" model, although the more usual term is "transient". These models attempt to track the climatic path Earth can be expected to follow, as we continue to disturb the carbon cycle.

Climate models face a fundamental problem of validation. These models can be run for periods in the past, to check (validate) how well they track the past. However, *they are built in order to project the future, and for this purpose can only be validated as the future arrives*. A satisfactory fit to past data is a necessary condition for acceptance as likely to project the future usefully. However, there is no sufficient test, other than to wait for the future to arrive. The moral is that these models may be more useful in helping us think about what *may* happen, than in telling us what *will* happen.

There are about a dozen different climate models all conforming to the general description given above, but differing in the details of their implementation. If a model gives result too far from the consensus of other models, its assumptions are rigorously examined to find the reason for the deviation, resulting in a general "consensus" amongst models. In Tables 2 and 3 the "All Eleven" column gives the full range across all eleven models examined. Naturally the limits on "All Eleven" are wider than the results reported for the two individual models.

These climate models are driven by the amount of ACO2 and other greenhouse gasses. This in turn is driven by releases of fossil CO2 that may lead to feed-back loops as carbon is sequestered or formerly sequestered carbon is released as ACO2.

The release of CO2 (and other greenhouse gasses) is typically driven by a range of "scenarios" such as rate of growth of GDP, changes in energy intensity, and adoption of low or fossil-free technologies. These are described, and the implications for greenhouse gas releases worked out, and fed into the models. This allows the likely impact of global warming to be "bracketed" between high and low impacts, resulting in the consensus view that by 2050 global temperature is likely to have risen between 1.5o C, and 4.0o C above the pre-industrial level (a fairly wide bracket).

Although not yet a part of the IPCC assessments there is interest in using "work horse" economic Computable General Equilibrium (CGE) models to study the impact of economic policies on the competitive position of alternative energy technologies, and thus on emissions of fossil CO2. Gan and Smith[40] used a comparative static, multi-sectoral and multiregional CGE model that allowed for energy substitution and hence CO2 emissions, emission trading and inter-sectoral linkages. This enabled them to estimate the extent of the CO2 reduction, or carbon taxes needed to make forest logging residues or specially planted poplar plantations competitive with coal. Some numerical results are reported in Chapter 7.

There is increasing interest amongst climate modelers in replacing their "scenarios" with linkages to economic CGE models predicting human behavior as reflected in economic activity[41]. Such models are described as *integrated models.*

This reflects the fact that global warming is an *economic problem.* Scenarios treat increases in fossil-CO2 as an exogenous variable. "It just happens", and is not in any-way connected to the dynamics of the model itself. It is now being recognized that this is ridiculous! If summer temperatures go up and last longer, is it not likely that air-conditioners will be run longer and AFCO2TA increased? If winter temperatures increase we may use less home heating and hope that AFCO2TA may decrease. There is no reason to expect these changes to cancel out, and in any case they can be swamped by consumer decisions to switch to nuclear electricity, more fuel efficient cars, and "personal virtue" energy savings.

Actual levels of AFCO2TA exceed the highest rates included in IPCC "scenarios" due to factors not included in the models, and this unexpectedly high level of AFCO2TA occurred in real time, not ten or twenty years in the future, when models could perhaps be forgiven for going off-track.

Integrated modeling is only in its infancy, but is clear that the most powerful feed-back loop from global warming is human behavior, it is after all human activity that is adding fossil carbon in the first place. Economists have a range of models (specifically Computable General Equilibrium, CGE, models) suitable for integrating with climate models, and key concepts necessary for such integration[42]. In the early rounds of working with such integrated models, numerical results may not be very meaningful, but the policy insights are likely to be invaluable. Notably the need to bring prices to bear in support of "personal virtue", and in tracing out the differential impact of cap and trade, as compared to a revenue neutral fossil carbon tax. Linkages within an integrated model need to be two-way, since climate change can impact economic activity, just as economic activity can impact ACO2.

As an example of the inevitable weakness of climate projection models, let us suppose that as the Earth warms, it triggers conditions to release the vast amount of methane hydrate currently sequestered in the deep ocean. Since this has not occurred in historic data series most models would not make allowance for this occurring, leading to major errors in their projections. Even models that provided for methane hydrate releases would be very lucky to have chosen the right trigger for this to occur.

Climate models are the best projection tool that we have, but they are far from perfect, as witness the number of times that climatic changes (particularly the break-up of the Antarctic ice-shelves) have happened faster than scientists expected, and the neglect of the global warming-human behavior feed-back loops. (For further discussion of modeling see Annex 8).

Economic Impact: The Stern Review and other economic analyses based on the IPCC models all project lower levels of economic activity (GDP) as a result of limiting AFCO2TA. This is plausible only if you assume no adverse economic effects from continuing to AFCO2TA. In fact the impact of higher levels of ACO2, in causing floods, droughts, hurricanes, forest fires, sea level rise, etc. is likely to impact GDP very adversely. Whereas replacing almost all power stations, replacing the electric grid, revitalizing public transport, etc., all necessary if we are to dispense with fossil fuels, is likely to induce a major Keynesian boom.

The Wedge Approach: In 2004, Stephen Pascala and Robert Socolow wrote a seminal paper in *Science*, showing how the apparently intractable problem of increasing rates of AFCO2TA could be broken down into a series of "doable" changes that would allow the rate of AFCO2TA to be stabilized at the 2004 level. It was, and is, an important paper, since it demonstrated how much could be done with existing technologies: We do not have to wait for the Bush-promised hydrogen revolution. The claim to rely only on existing technologies may be overly optimistic, given their reliance on CO2 sequestration and hydrogen, neither of which can yet strictly be described as an "existing technology". Be that as it may, Stephen Pascala and Robert Socolow clearly illustrate the difference between a technical/scientific approach to the problem of global warming, and an economic/policy approach.

As a minor critical note, Pascala and Socolow identified the problem as *stabilizing* the rate of AFCO2TA, (that would imply a steady increase in the concentration of ACO2) rather than *eliminating* AFCO2TA. No matter, they would just have had to identify more "wedges".

The key idea presented by Pascala and Socolow was that the apparently impossible task of halving the rate of AFCO2TA compared to what it would be under "business as usual" (BAU) in 2054, could be broken down into fifteen technical "wedges" such as:

1. Double efficiency of 2 billion cars from 30 mpg to 60 mpg.

2. Decrease the number of miles traveled by car by 50%.

3. Use best efficiency practices in all residential and commercial buildings.

4. Double the efficiency of coal based power plants.

5. Replace 1,400 coal based electricity generating plants, with natural gas plants.

6. Capture and store emissions from 800 coal-fired electric generating plants.

7. Produce hydrogen from coal at six times today's rates, and store the captured CO2.

8. Capture the carbon from 180 coal-to-synfuel plants and store the CO2.

9. Double the nuclear electric generating capacity to replace coal-based generation.

10. Increase wind generator capacity by 50-times (for a total of 2 million large windmills).

11. Install 700 times the current capacity of solar electricity.

12. Use 40,000 square kilometers of solar panels (or 4 million windmills) to produce hydrogen for cars.

13. Increase ethanol production by 50 times by creating biomass plantations, with area equal to one sixth of the world's croplands.

14. Eliminate tropical deforestation and establish new plantations on non-forested land for a four-fold increase in plantation area.

15. Adopt conservation tillage in all agricultural soils world-wide[43].

These wedges are calculated on a ceterus paribus (all other things equal) basis. As a result they are not additive, and more than 15 wedges may be needed to achieve stability (let alone to eliminate AFCO2TA).

Taking the first two wedges, doubling the fuel efficacy of cars, would produce the same saving as halving the mileage driven. Pascala and Socolow count each as a "wedge". However if we adopted both policies we would end up with saving not two wedges, but only one and a half. Having adopted wedge #1, cars would have a fuel efficiency of 60 mpg. Implementing wedge #2, by halving distance driven would have only half the saving (for cars doing 60 mpg) then would be yielded if cars were still at their initial mpg of 30.

Having identified the existence of these "wedges" Pascala and Socolow's job is done. They have told us it can be done technically, end of story.

This stands in stark contrast to the economic or policy approach that asks: What does government need to do to ensure that the fuel efficiency of 2 billion cars is doubled from 30 mpg to 60 by 2054? With similar questions for the other fourteen wedges.

Given the first wedge objective, several policy suggestions come to mind:

i)   Raise gas prices through a tax,

ii) Require an increasing proportion of a manufactures sales to be plug-in hybrids, (possibly, because economists love markets, a hybrid credit market where a manufacturer exceeding his target hybrid sales could sell rights to a manufacture who was lagging),

iii) Have annual mpg tests, and progressively raise the minimum mpg allowed for a car to be registered,

iv) Have annual mpg tests, with higher road taxes for lower mpg cars.

While policies designed to double mpg can be readily suggested, the policies required for other wedges may not exist. It is hard to see, for instance, how governments could ensure the adoption of "conservation tillage in all agricultural soils worldwide".

Reviewing the fifteen wedges, three of them require capture and sequestration of CO_2, and two of them involve producing hydrogen. No doubt the hydrogen could be produced and used as a simple fuel (wedge # 7), but as discussed in Chapter 9, this still leaves numerous technical problems to be resolved before the hydrogen car (wedge #12) will be a feasible replacement for the hybrid.

Stephen Pascala and Robert Socolow's paper has probably influenced the subsequent allocation of research monies. In particular it may have resulted in higher priority for research related to the hydrogen economy, and sequestration of CO_2. As discussed in Chapter 9, these may not be good choices. The only policy initiative consistent with the 15 wedges is President Bush's objective of increasing fuel efficiency by 20 percent in 10 years announced in his State of the Union address for 2007. This leaves 14 wedges unaddressed, and almost certainty that stabilizing (never mind eliminating) the rate of AFCO2TA by 2054 will not be achieved.

Chapter 3.   Personal Virtue

Questioned about the role of conservation in his recommended energy policy, Vice President Cheney said that "conservation may be a sign of personal virtue, but it is not a sufficient basis for a sound, comprehensive energy policy". Be that as it may, fortunately there are a growing number of people who feel led to help minimize the impact of global warming by reducing their use of fossil fuels.

There is a whole laundry list of things we can do to as individuals to stop AFCO2TA:

- Replace incandescent bulbs with florescent

- Buy a smaller, preferably hybrid, car

- Use public transport when available

- Buy local rather than inter-state or international produce

- Buy energy efficient appliances

- Have a vegetable garden

- Install photo-voltaic roof panels

- Turn off unneeded lights and appliances

- Install solar-water heating

- Turn down the thermostat in winter

- Turn up the thermostat in summer

- Add insulation

- Walk rather than drive

- Car pool where possible

- Limit air travel

- Buy fossil-free electricity

- Use an electric lawn-mower or chain-saw

- Use wood fires

- Wear wool in winter, and, or course

- Shower with a friend.

These are all helpful and valid things to do. However there is a limit to what can be achieved by even the most rigorous application of this approach. When all is said and done even the hybrid car uses some gasoline, the florescent light still uses some electricity (about 25% of that used by incandescent bulbs), the local power company may not supply fossil free electricity, even the adjusted thermostat allows the heating/air conditioning to come on sporadically, and there may be no practical alternative to air travel.

In addition to practicing personal virtue in daily living, it is also open to people acting as individuals to practice personal virtue in their investment decisions. Presumably, at some stage, fossil-free mutual funds will be on offer, in the mean time individuals can look for investment opportunities in such areas as:

- Wind Farms

- Bio-diesel

- Bio-ethanol[44]

- Photo-voltaics

- Nuclear power

- Solar-thermal

And of course by avoiding investments such as air-lines and fossil fuel producers.

As a practical example of what personal virtue can actual achieve consider the Tidwell House[45]. By a series of hardware and lifestyle changes Mike Tidwell has almost erased the carbon footprint of his house in Baltimore.

Most impressively Mike Tidwell's house is not a one-off custom built demonstration home, but a modest 1915 home with a small yard. Hardware changes have included:

- A solar water heater on the roof,

- Photo-voltaic panels on the roof,

- Window air conditioner,

- Ceiling Fans (the 1915 house has nice high ceilings),

- An energy efficient refrigerator,

- Florescent light bulbs,

- A corn-burning stove, has replaced the (natural gas) furnace.

The corn-burning stove has a storage bin that can take seventy pounds of corn. The corn is augured automatically into the fire, as needed over a two-day period. The stove is on the ground-floor and with the help of the ceiling fans heats the whole house.

The refrigerator is an "energy star" model that cost $150 more than less efficient models, but uses only a third the electricity of the model it replaced. The photo-voltaic panels produce excess electricity on summer days. Under Maryland law this domestically produced electricity can be sold to the grid (the electric meter actually runs backwards!) at the same price that electricity is sold to consumers. This offsets a large portion of night-time electricity requirements.

Key behavior modification has focused on eliminating "electricity leakage", that is appliances left on (such as computers, or DVDs) when not in use, and turning off lights not being used.

The Tidwell house is not totally fossil free. Mike uses about 40% of the natural gas he used to for supplemental water heating, and about $200 of fossil free electricity a year, without any decline in his standard of living.

Mike was very canny in purchasing his hardware, buying the roof-top water heater second-hand, and taking advantage of a Maryland grant program in the purchase of his photo-voltaic cells, and installing much of the hardware himself.

Not many people are in a position to build from scratch, but we need to be aware of the great scope for reducing the use of residential energy. *Passivhaus*[46] is a design concept developed in Germany in the late 80's, that requires neither central heating nor air conditioning. Key design features are good insulation, air-tight construction, and no "thermal bridges" that would conduct heat from the house to the exterior, or vica versa. Given the key role of an airtight construction in preventing energy leaks (in or out), provision needs to be made to provide fresh air, thus fresh-air is pumped into the house after heat exchange with outgoing air, and possibly heat exchange with the soil, and the entire air supply is renewed every three or four hours.

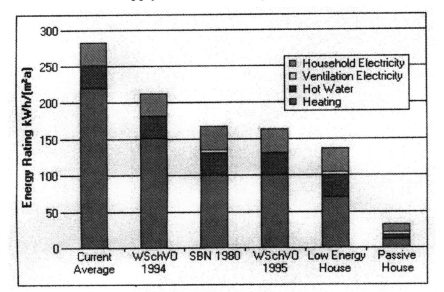

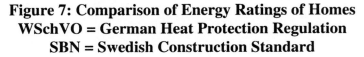

Figure 7: Comparison of Energy Ratings of Homes
WSchVO = German Heat Protection Regulation
SBN = Swedish Construction Standard

While not the complete answer, it is surprising how much can be achieved one house, or family, at a time.

In the United States, there is an active NGO architecture2030.org that points out that 76% of all electricity produced by coal plants is consumer in buildings. If all new and renovated buildings conformed to increasingly stringent energy standards, there would be no need to build any new coal plants. Architecture2030.org has been successful in getting many municipalities to adopt the 2030 Challenge[47]. There is indeed much that can be done, *using existing technologies.*

California leads the nation in public (state and utilities) support for personal virtue. From 2000 to 2004, Californian utilities spent $1.4 billion to encourage more efficient use of electricity. The average cost of the electricity saved was 2.9 cents per kilowatt-hour, as compared to 16.7 cents per hour to generate peak power and 5.8 cents to generate base load power. Californian electricity rates are about 50% higher than the national average, while power consumption is only 7,000 kilowatt-hours per person, as compared to the national average of 13,000 kilowatt hours per person[48]. This demonstrates capacity of individual to adjust when prompted by higher prices, and supported by guidance from their utility company[49].

Historically, in the face of very much higher oil prices (the "oil crisis") from 1973 to 1983 US consumption of oil held constant even as the economy grew: Given the right price signals, demand adjusts.

Personal virtue also occurs "one firm at a time". A recent NYTimes article[50] recounts the "conversion experience" of a Mr. Ray Anderson, CEO of a carpet company, who in reading about environmental issues found that his company was a major and unnecessary polluter. As a result of this conversion experience, Mr. Anderson took a completely fresh look at the operations of his company, under the main heading of:

- Waste Elimination: This included physical waste, but also miss-directed shipments, incorrect invoices, the lot. Physical waste was dramatically reduced by redesigning processes to reduce off-cuts, and using the remaining off-cuts wherever possible as raw material for other processes. Over a decade this led to cumulative saving of about $350 million.

- Benign Emissions: By reusing waste-water one factory was able to reduce water consumption by 30%, a $10,000 a year saving. Chemical use was also analyzed this allowed all chemicals requiring mandatory reporting to EPA to be eliminated.

- Renewable Energy: The company is supporting markets for renewable energy, testing technologies, installing renewable energy systems, and establishing renewable energy purchasing targets. Photovoltaic panels have been installed in some facilities. Carbon credits are also used (but hopefully these will be phased out, see Chapter 4 for a critique of carbon credits).

- Recycling: They have reduced the amount of raw material used by careful recycling of synthetic materials so that waste materials in society become valuable raw materials in industry. They also seek to keep organic materials uncontaminated so they may return to their natural systems. From 1995 to 2006 the Company has gone from about 1 percent recycled and biological raw material to about 20 percent.

- Transportation: This is a very difficult area, since the technical alternatives are not numerous. They place heavy reliance on carbon credits to offset emissions that they cannot avoid (again see reservations discussed in the next chapter). They have facilitated ride-sharing for employee commutes, and very innovatively seek to teleconference rather travel whenever possible.

- Energizing People: The Company has fostered an open, cooperative spirit in the organization, empowering all employees to make suggestions as to how processes could be improved. They have organized meeting with suppliers and customers, to solicit suggestions as to how suppliers and customers could make their own savings.

- Redesigning Commerce: The Company has also introduced the idea of leasing carpet, this has the advantage that worn carpet comes automatically back to the company for reworking, and for the customer that worn areas are constantly maintained.

Individuals can have a huge impact through personal virtue, especially if they take a wide view of what is under their control.

Valuable though personal virtue is, it cannot be relied upon as a "policy" since it is unrealistic to expect everyone to practice it. Even if everyone practiced personal virtue, most would still need to use some fossil fuel. This leads naturally to the idea of idea of "carbon neutrality".

Chapter 4:   Carbon Neutrality[51]

Carbon neutrality is a very attractive idea: Namely that when we absolutely have to use fossil fuels, we can buy a carbon credit, representing an equivalent saving of carbon, made by someone else. There are a large number of firms offering carbon credits. To see a selection of carbon credit suppliers google "carbon credits" or go to http://www.ecobusinesslinks.com/carbon_offset_wind_credits_ carbon_reduction.htm[52], or see Annex 1.

Carbon neutrality is an idea that does not stand up well to closer scrutiny. Carbon credits are of three major types. The first offers to sequester carbon in biomass to offset releases of fossil-carbon. Basically this equates *shifting* some bio-carbon within the carbon cycle from ACO2 to biomass with *adding* fossil carbon to the cycle. Clearly this is a non-starter, since we cannot know how long it will take the sequestered carbon to take the next step in the cycle and return to the atmosphere.

A second approach is to claim a carbon credit for an activity that adds to the carbon cycle but less intensively than would have been possible. For example, it might be claimed that replacing an incandescent bulb by a florescent bulb, gave the same light, but used much less (fossil) electricity. Again this does not bear analysis. To offset my *adding* carbon to the cycle, I need someone to *remove* carbon from the cycle. That would be a true offset, but this is nowhere in sight. In essence this type of offset argues that *because someone did not use the dirtiest technology, they have created carbon credits*. The florescent bulb is still AFCO2TA, just not as much as the alternative technology. Since almost anything we do could be done in a more energy intensive way, almost anything we do could be claimed to generate carbon credits and the supply of carbon credits is endless.

For sake of argument, let us assume that it would be valid to give carbon credit equivalent to fossil-carbon emissions avoided. Suppose I planned to fly to Europe, but changed my mind. Clearly this change of mind reduces the emissions that would have resulted from my planned flight. So by changing my mind, I have created carbon credits? You want to fly to Europe while maintaining a carbon neutral life style? Easy, plan on two trips, cancel the second, and the carbon credits generated from the cancellation can be used to offset the fossil carbon emissions generated by the trip you actually take. (It is stupid, but that is the "logic" of emissions-avoided carbon credits.)

Suppose that there was an upper limit, of say 100 flights to Europe. In this case if you bought two tickets and tore up one of them, something real would have been achieved --- only 99 flights would now be possible. (Whether you could still consider you were being carbon neutral in using one of the remaining tickets is by no means self-evident). Creating carbon credits in the absence of a limit makes no sense. The person selling a carbon credit is at liberty to use the income to buy another electrical appliance that will AFCO2TA. We have no idea what the outcome of buying such carbon credits will be.

A third approach is to suggest that use of fossil-free electricity should generate carbon credits. But again, the purchaser of the carbon credit would do so because they were *adding* carbon to the cycle. An offset requires someone to *remove* carbon from the cycle (not just shift it within the cycle). But even *fossil-free electricity does not remove carbon from the carbon cycle* it merely refrains from adding it. Even if valid, we immediately have a problem, who should get the credits? The investor who creates a wind-farm? The wind-farm that sells the fossil-free electricity? Or, the consumer who buys it?

Clearly each has an equally valid (or invalid) claim:

i)   The investor can claim that he *built* a fossil-free generator,

ii) The operating wind farm can claim that it *sold* fossil-free electricity (Annex 4), and

iii) The purchaser can claim that she *bought* fossil-free electricity, where she could have bought fossil-electricity.

Perhaps we should create three carbon credits for each unit of electricity?

The problem is that there is no matter how much fossil-free electricity is generated, *this does not remove carbon from the cycle.* Clearly the person who uses fossil-free electricity does not need a carbon offset, since she has not caused carbon to be added to the cycle, in the first place.

Many of the actions/arguments used to generate carbon credits are excellent actions totally to be encouraged, and of high priority as contributing to personal virtue. Use of energy efficient light-bulbs and appliances, use of wind or nuclear power, use of a hybrid car, planting trees, limiting international travel, etc, etc, are all highly commendable life-style changes since they reduce (or eliminate) AFCO2TA for the activity: *But they do not remove carbon from the cycle.*

Carbon credits come with a story: This carbon credit was generated because someone took a given action, lets say they used an energy efficient light bulb. Over the life of the bulb it will save x amount of carbon.

People buy carbon credits in the belief that they are offsetting actions that AFCO2TA, that they cannot (or do not wish to) avoid. But on examination, no carbon credit will be found to *remove* the carbon from the carbon cycle, *added* to the cycle by AFCO2TA. (Some such as planting trees may temporarily *move* it within the cycle, but they do not *remove* it). Buying a carbon credit makes the purchaser feel good: The carbon neutral life style is better described as a "feel good" life style, with little or no effect on AFCO2TA.

Lest the above seem overly cynical, it may be of interest to consider four examples of carbon credits contributing to this $100 million industry.

Four types of carbon offsets are on offer:

i) Totally bogus,

ii) Sequestering carbon in biological form, such as trees,

iii) Reduced (fossil) CO2 emissions due to lifestyle changes, as in the use of florescent bulbs, and

iv) Investment in fossil-free energy generation such as wind-farms or bio-ethanol.

Undertaken as personal virtue, each of the carbon credit generating activities, may be highly commendable, but they do not *remove* carbon from the cycle.

A Totally Bogus Scheme: In this project cow manure was broken down in an anaerobic digester to yield methane, that was then burned to generate electricity.

O.K. What is wrong with this scheme? Well, the carbon in the cow manure that is the basis for this scheme is *bio-carbon*. It comes from grass or corn that was fed to the animal, and the carbon in the grass or corn was recently *withdrawn* from the atmosphere by photosynthesis.

A valid (if not very attractive scheme) would claim to *sequester the carbon as cow manure* (perhaps in huge underground caverns?) *never allowing the contained carbon to return to the atmosphere.* Instead, by producing and burning the methane the scheme *sells "carbon credits" equivalent to the CO2 being returned to the atmosphere!* (sic).

If the cattle were free-range, their manure would drop on the pasture, acting as a fertilizer as it decomposed. Contained nitrogen, phosphate and potassium would serve to fertilize the grass, while carbon would be *returned* to the atmosphere as CO2 as the manure decayed (was consumed by micro-organisms). This is the natural carbon cycle.

When cattle are housed, substantial manure is produced in one place that may be taken out and spread on fields (imitating the natural cycle) or stored in lagoons, where it may decay under anaerobic processes producing methane.

The scheme involves capturing this methane and harvesting the energy by burning it, thus completing the cycle to return CO2 to the atmosphere. This is an efficient way of harvesting the energy in manure, but does nothing to offset fossil-carbon releases. With or without the digester, the same amount of carbon will be *returned* to the atmosphere.

But wait! Isn't there another line of argument? Cannot we argue that the energy created by burning the bio-methane, saved burning coal (or natural gas) to generate the same energy? No! Otherwise you would give carbon credits every time wood was burnt, not to mention the millions of Indian peasants who regularly burn cow manure as fuel. *You cannot offset fossil-carbon emissions by modifying the carbon cycle*, or claiming that you could have replaced bio-carbon with fossil.

The scheme is mind-boggling stupid (although no doubt highly profitable): Since I feel guilty about driving my SUV, I buy carbon offsets. Step one is to calculate how many pounds of fossil carbon my driving habit releases to the atmosphere. Using the cow-dung scheme, I then pay for bio-carbon that was sequestered (albeit for a short time) in cow-dung, to be released to the atmosphere. If the calculations are done right, for every pound of fossil carbon released by my driving I pay for another pound of bio-carbon to be released, thus *doubling* the CO2 released to the atmosphere by my driving (and purchase of an offset).[53]

Annex 2, has the project verification statement. Note that bio-carbon dioxide and bio-methane were treated as "air pollutants" in the verification, and the carbon credit was achieved by burning methane to *release* carbon dioxide. At the end of the day, this scheme *creates* carbon credits by releasing carbon dioxide to the atmosphere (sic).

It can be argued that the digester results in less methane (a strong greenhouse gas) in the carbon cycle. But it is the farming system that artificially concentrates cattle and fails to return dung to the field that creates the methane in the first place. A reversion to free-range grazing would dispense with the need for a digester. Moreover there is *no equivalence* between AFCO2TA and accelerating by a few months the time bio-carbon will be converted to bio-CO2 within the normal working of the carbon cycle.

There are numerous horror stories, where, for instance, *rather than plant trees, the carbon trading company merely bought the rights to the carbon emissions of existing trees!*[54] In this case there clearly was no offset, although a gullible public paid the carbon trading company for "carbon credits", and no doubt "felt good about it". Clearly there is no limit to the carbon credits that can be generated if existing forests (the Amazon, Congo?) are conceived as generating currently unclaimed carbon credits.

But wait again! Could it not be argued that in the absence of the carbon credits, the trees would have been cut down? If so, why not claim carbon credits for the tree as well as its annual uptake of ACO2? The whole thing is wall to wall snake oil.

Note however, that *the technology of burning methane generated within the carbon cycle, does provide fossil free energy, and is a useful activity if undertaken by the farmer as a matter of personal virtue.* It just cannot be used to offset fossil carbon *added* to the atmosphere by a transatlantic flight.

Biological Sequestration: The idea here is that (bio)-carbon can be sequestered (stored) in plants, thus removing it from the atmosphere for the duration of the sequestering. Trees, because of their long life, are a favorite for biological sequestering, although the same argument could be made for sequestering in an annual crop, and even for plankton[55].

Remember that fossil-carbon added to the atmosphere is added *permanently*: It is added to the carbon in the carbon cycle with no half-life for decaying back into fossil-carbon. Thus any true offset has to sequester a corresponding amount of bio-carbon *permanently.* Moreover, it has to be a sequestration *that would not otherwise have occurred.* We cannot have farmers selling carbon credits for planting corn on land that has been in corn for years, and would remain in corn in the absence of the offset. There has, at a minimum, to be *a real change in sequestration to generate a carbon credit.*

In another scheme sold by carbonfund.org trees were planted in an area damaged by forest fire, where it was alleged that trees would not regenerate on their own. To get the trees planted carbonfund.org worked with project developers, implying that there was little likelihood that the selected area would be left unplanted, in any case. It was acknowledged that carbonfund.org would only take an interest in the plantings until "the end of the project".

Lets take a look at this scheme at its face value. The forest won't regenerate on it's own (and presumably no one will help it regenerate in the absence of the project). So we get a movement within the carbon cycle, equivalent to the forest's growth, *until the next forest fire:* And then nothing. So we have a *permanent* addition of fossil-carbon "offset" by a *temporary* sequestration (movement within the cycle) of bio-carbon. These are apples and oranges. No information is provided as to how they are equated.

Neglecting the problem of forest fires, and assuming the land would have remained neglected in perpetuity, what is the probability that the forest once established will be left intact in perpetuity? Carbonfund.org does not pretend to maintain an interest beyond "the life of the project". Anyway it is again equating additions of carbon to the cycle with movements within the cycle.

Again, as a matter of personal (or national) virtue planting forests and protecting them is highly commendable, but it provides no offset against a transatlantic flight.

Life-Style Changes: The idea here is that if my old (or planned) life-style would have generated x tons of carbon, but I make changes so that only y tons are produced, I should earn carbon credits for the x-y tons expected/planned to be produced, but not produced. An example would be a house with incandescent lights that has them replaced by fluorescents, so that the electricity used for lighting is reduced by 75%. Should this qualify for a carbon credit? No! Where is the carbon *removed* from the cycle?

Again, as a matter of personal virtue, reduced carbon releases due to changed light-bulbs or efficient appliances are to be commended, but they do not provide an offset against transatlantic flights.

Consider a third carbonfund.org scheme the Zero-Energy Solar Home project. The project involved the construction of seven energy efficient affordable homes, including unspecified "advanced technologies to reduce energy demand" and photovoltaic roof panels to reduce the demand for electricity from the grid.

What is going on here? Seven homes are to be built that will use only 25% of the energy of conventional homes without photo-voltaic panels. The net result is AFCO2TA. The 25% of conventional energy used *adds* fossil CO_2 to the atmosphere; and this generates a carbon credit, because *the addition could have been even greater*? Remind me, what are we trying to do here? Where is there carbon *removed* from the cycle?

This leads to the problem at the core of concept of "carbon neutrality": *At the end of the day, carbon credit in hand, the purchaser has not been carbon neutral*[56]. He took the trip to Europe thus adding fossil-carbon to the atmosphere. There is no getting away from it. This is in marked contrast to "personal virtue" where the individual takes actions (even perhaps forgoing a holiday in Europe) that directly reduce fossil carbon emissions.

Fossil-Free Energy: This leaves investing in fossil-free energy production. Assuming that you succeed in building a wind-farm that does indeed generate fossil free energy, where is the *reduction* in carbon from the cycle? Yes more fossil free energy has been produced, but where is the assurance that AFCO2TA has been *reduced*? Maybe we just have more energy in total. Again as a matter of personal (or company) virtue fossil-free energy production is to be greatly encouraged, but as a method of *removing* carbon from the cycle, it just does not cut it.

There is also a question of timing of the offset. Annex 3 provides a detailed analysis of a carbon offset, showing that if trees are used to generate the carbon credit, it may be a 100 years before the added fossil-carbon is sequestered ("moved within the cycle" and as we have seen above, there is no knowing how long this sequestration will last). In the mean time, the unsequestered fossil-carbon will be contributing to global warming. Not something to feel good about.

Carbon credits are ridiculously cheap. At www.mycarbondebt.com you can buy an offset for a return trans-Atlantic flight (1.5 tonnes of carbon) for L17.62 (17.62 pounds sterling), about \$35.25[57]. If only global warming could be avoided at such a low cost! Obviously something is wrong with the whole carbon credit/carbon neutral scheme, as argued above.

Green Cards: Credit card companies are also getting into the act. In addition to offering airline miles or cash back for use of their cards, companies including G.E., Barclay's Bank (in the U.K.), Rabobank (in Holland) and Bank of America (in the U.S.) they are now offering to a range of "green" credit cards. Details differ, but the banks offer to invest a portion of their profits in carbon reduction projects or to buy offsetting carbon credits. None of these offerings will actual remove carbon from the carbon cycle they will merely shift carbon within the cycle, having no long term beneficial effect. No doubt they will be a commercial success as "feel good" cards.

There is an error of composition in the carbon neutral life style: Yes an individual can (conceptually) follow such a life style: Provided others do not. If I am to buy a valid carbon credit, there has to be someone to sell it to me. That is someone who is *not* following a carbon neutral lifestyle.

For carbon credits to be valid, the vendor has to be limited in the amount of fossil carbon he can emit. In this case, if the vendor genuinely reduces his emissions in order to generate the credit, it can be reasonably argued that a real reduction in AFCO2TA has occurred, thus providing a valid offset. However, most privately traded carbon credits (those that underpin the carbon neutral life-style) are generated in situations where there is no limitation on the amount of fossil carbon the vendor can use. The person who sells a carbon credit for plugging in a florescent bulb is free to install additional lights in the house with bulbs of his choosing, or indeed to discontinue using the florescent bulb.

It is encouraging that people's concern about global warming can generate a $100 million industry on such fabrications. It is discouraging that well intentioned people can be so easily deceived (or perhaps self-deceiving?). Some authors have referred to carbon credits as "greenwash", they reassure people that they can continue using fossil fuels, but feel they are nevertheless achieving carbon neutrality.

People as prominent and well informed as Al Gore and Tony Blair, when accused of extravagant energy use, have resorted to buying carbon credits as an offset. This suggests they really do not understand the problem.

All of this said carbon credits contain the nucleus of a good idea. If the money was used for schemes that withdrew CO_2 from the atmosphere and sequestered it *permanently*, then a valid offset would have been generated. At the moment the best that could be hoped for is that money would be used to support research, development and demonstration that withdrawal of CO_2 from the atmosphere and permanent sequestration are even technically feasible.

Chapter 5:   Clean Coal, Energy Independence and Methane Hydrate

"Clean coal" and "energy independence" are two ideas supported by the American coal lobby. The first is that coal can be made "clean", and the second that coal can be used to make gasoline, and thus free America from its dependence on imported oil.

According to Wikipedia[58]:

"Clean coal is the name attributed to coal chemically washed of minerals and impurities, sometimes gasified, burned and the resulting flue gases treated with steam, with the purpose of almost completely eradicating sulfur, and reburned so as to make the carbon dioxide in the flue gas economically recoverable. The coal industry uses the term clean coal to describe technologies designed to enhance both the efficiency and the environmental acceptability of coal extraction, preparation and use, with no specific quantitative limits on any emissions, particularly carbon dioxide.

….The concept of clean coal as a solution to climate change and global warming is claimed to be 'greenwash' by some environmental organizations such as Greenpeace because emissions and wastes are not avoided, but are transferred from one waste stream to another. The Australian of The Year, renowned scientist and author Tim Flannery has been reported as saying 'Coal can't be clean'.

There are no coal fired power stations in commercial production which capture all carbon dioxide emissions, so the process is theoretical and experimental and thus a subject of feasibility or pilot studies. It is estimated that it will be 2020 to 2025 before any commercial scale clean coal power stations (coal burning power stations with carbon capture and sequestration) are commercially viable and widely adopted. This time frame is of concern because there is an urgent and immediate need to mitigate greenhouse gas emissions and climate change to protect the world economy according to the Stern report. Even when CO_2 emissions can be caught, there is considerable debate over the necessary carbon capture and storage that must follow.

Box 2: CO_2 Capture and Sequestration (CCS)

Carbon dioxide capture and sequestration has been demonstrated where the CO_2 is pumped into a depleted oil field, to force the remaining oil to the surface:

At <u>Sleipner T</u> (a Norwegian Statoil, oil-rig in the North Sea) an excess Supply of CO_2 is bled off natural gas (to reduce CO_2 content to 2%) before sale. The CO_2 is then injected into the ground, 1,000 meters below the sea bed. StatOil has been sequestering CO_2 in this way since 1997. This is in response to a tax of $50 per ton of carbon dioxide ($ 13.60 per ton of carbon).

The <u>In Salah</u> field in Algeria, is quite similar to Sleipner T, in that the CO_2 is stripped from natural gas to bring CO_2 content to a level acceptable for export (0.3%), and that Statoil is a partner in the project. The CO_2 is injected into an aquifer, in order to force residual oil to the surface.

The <u>Weyburn</u> project is intended to demonstrate, by 2010, that CO_2-Enhanced Oil Recovery is economically viable, environmentally responsible and socially acceptable. Weyburn, is located in southeastern Saskatchewan, near the U.S. border with North Dakota. CO_2 recovered from a Synfuels financed coal gasification plant in North Dakota is piped 200 miles across the border to Weyburn, and injected into a partially depleted oil field. This is subsidized by the Canadian government and is intended to establish the degree of security with which CO_2 can be stored in geological formations during large-scale, commercial, enhanced oil-recovery operations.

The US Department of Energy (DOE) is supporting <u>FutureGen</u> an initiative to build the world's first zero-emissions coal power plant. When operational, in 2012, the $ 1 billion prototype is intended to be the cleanest fossil fuel fired power plant in the world. It is a significant part of the DOE's research program.

When coal is burnt, it produces CO2. That much is clear. To qualify as "clean" it is necessary that the CO2 be *captured*, and *sequestered*. There are four cases where CO2 is being captured and sequestered (see Box 2). Note that none of these examples reflect private sector electrical generation. Thus what we have to deal with are designs, rather than operating plants. A recent study from MIT[59] analyses a range of coal-generation plant designs, with and without carbon capture. The overall conclusions are:

i) In the absence of a charge for CO2 releases (either in the form of a tax, or as a result of cap-and-trade (C&T)) carbon capture is uneconomic,

ii) The energy required for carbon capture reduces the energy efficiency of electricity production by about 33%,

iii) Cost of electricity production is increased by about 40% with carbon capture,

iv) Carbon capture breaks even with a carbon tax of about $110 per ton of carbon released, and

v) Building a plant without capture, but ready to have carbon capture added is financially unattractive. Better to build a plant without capture and pay the penalty, or build a plant with capture, but not operate the capture until a fee is charged.

While the alternative design options are generally agreed, and some plants (without carbon capture) are under constructions, there is little actual operating experience, so that the above results are from comparative design studies, rather than empirical results averaged across many operating plants.

The cleanest (most efficient) generator design without carbon capture is <u>pulverized coal (PC)</u>: Where very finely ground coal is burnt. This promises to raise thermal efficiency from about 40% to 55%, allowing less coal to be used per unit of electricity generated. The problem is, of course that although less coal is being used fossil carbon (admittedly *less* fossil carbon) is still being added to the atmosphere[60].

Carbon Capture and Sequestration (CCS). The CO_2 from a pulverized coal plant can separated from the flue gasses, and then sequestered. This is difficult since CO_2 is only a small part of the flue gasses.

Integrated Gasification Combined-Cycle (IGCC) where the coal is first turned into gas before using it to generate electricity. In this case the flue gasses are predominantly CO_2 and hydrogen that are easily separated. IGCC can also be used without carbon capture, but this is more expensive than the simpler pulverized coal design.

The MIT study recommends an intensive program of RD&D (Research, Development and Demonstration) focusing on commercial generation using the range of available designs for electricity generation *with carbon capture.*

"Carbon capture" is only half the story, the captured CO_2 also has to be sequestered. In principle carbon could be sequestered as CO_2 hydrate in the deep ocean, which already houses more carbon, as methane hydrate, than in the entire inventory of fossil fuels. The relevant technology for sequestering CO_2 has not yet been developed[61]. (However work on *releasing energy, and hence carbon*, from methane hydrate is comparatively well advanced, see below).

Practical proposals for sequestration involve storage in geological formations. Initial interest has been in depleted oil fields, since injection of CO_2 can be used to enhance oil recovery, and the geology of depleted field is well known. A second promising formation is saline formations with saline water in the pores of the rock. Deep coal seams also hold promise. All told these formations are thought to have the capacity to store hundreds and perhaps thousands of gigatons of CO_2: So potential storage sites do not appear to be a problem.

Experience with natural gas and oil, leads geologists to be confident that short term leakage from these geological formations can be avoided. There is insufficient experience to be able to properly judge the likely extent of long term leakage. At present even identifying in a timely manner that leakage into the atmosphere or ground water is occurring cannot be guaranteed, let alone taking remedial measures.

The MIT report argues strongly for regulation and inspection of proposed sequestration sites. Absent independent supervision, there would be a strong incentive for companies to cut corners, hoping that releases would not occur, or that the company would be able to walk away from any eventual damage. Given that sites would be inspected and approved by government, it seems sensible that in the event of CO_2 releases companies should be charged at half the rate for direct emission to the atmosphere[62], but that for this reduced penalty, limited liability for shareholders should be removed.

Transport of captured CO_2 to the sequestration site would be by pipeline, and is expected to add 20% to the cost of capture and compression. However, this cost will be highly variable depending on the distance to the sequestration site, the volume of CO_2 to be sequestered and the terrain to be traversed by the pipeline.

In short, "clean coal" with CO_2 capture and sequestration appears to be technically possible, although not yet demonstrated (It is not until 2012 that the U.S. Department of Energy hopes to have its first emission free power plant, *FutureGen*, fully operational.) A carbon tax of about $140 per ton, would be bring the costs of clean coal into line with dirty coal. To make clean coal substantially more profitable, the tax would need to be substantially greater than $140 per ton.

The danger with clean coal is that the promise of eventual "emission free coal power plants", will lull policy makers into believing that since we will eventually be able to build clean coal plants, we can for the moment continue to build dirty ones. Whereas *the correct policy recommendation for developed countries is a moratorium on coal generation plants pending the promised development of truly clean coal plants, with zero greenhouse gas emissions.*

The MIT study clearly shows that building dirty coal plants designed to be retrofit with carbon capture technology is likely to be less profitable that building dirty plants and paying the tax, or building carbon capture plants initially and waiting for the tax to become effective. (This conclusion rests, of course, on the MIT assumption of a quite modest tax or trade price, to be introduced in 2015 or 2025.)

Energy independence, is a political policy aimed at eliminating the need for energy imports by the United States from beyond North America, or possibly this hemisphere. The idea is that this would remove the threat of oil shortage due to political instability in the Middle East, or Africa; or indeed from a natural or terrorist induced break down in the supply network. It is an essential policy if the U.S. is to remain the sole hyper-power.

Table 5: Change in Carbon Emissions for Non-Oil Petroleum

Technology	Change* (%)
Fossil Free Electricity	-100
Cellulosic Ethanol	-91
Bio-diesel	-68
Sugar Ethanol	-56
Electricity from Coal	-47
Gaseous Hydrogen	-41
Compressed Natural Gas	-29
Corn Ethanol	-22
Liquefied Petroleum Gas	-20
Methanol	- 9
Oil	0
Coal-to-Liquid with Carbon Sequestration	4
Liquid Hydrogen	7
Gas to Liquid Diesel	9
Coal-to-Liquid without Carbon Sequestration	119

*Percent change relative to oil. Source EPA.

There are a wide range of technologies ranging from plug-in hybrid cars through various forms of ethanol and bio-diesel, to hydrogen and "coal-to-liquid" with or without sequestering the CO2 emitted in preparing the petroleum substitute. The EPA has been looking at the alternative ways oil could be replaced in the production of petroleum, and in particular how this would affect releases of AFCO2TA. Table 5 shows the results.

Electricity is not a perfect substitute for petroleum since it implies a plug-in hybrid car, and could only be used for the first twenty miles of a journey, but for those twenty miles the percentages would apply. All the technologies with negative percentages would help reduce AFCO2TA if used to reduce dependence on imported oil. The four technologies with positive percentages would *increase* AFCO2TA (and make global warming worse). Carbon sequestration has already been discussed. Even with sequestration coal-to-liquid makes global warming slightly worse at the same time that it is being used to replace imported oil.

Coal-to-liquid *without sequestration* more than doubles the rate of AFCO2TA, as compared to the petrol that it would replace. As with clean coal, there is a danger that because sequestration on a large scale is expected to be technically possible within ten years, it will be argued that therefore we can safely proceed to develop coal-to-liquid plants without sequestration in the mean time. Given the doubling of the rate of AFCO2TA that this policy implies, it should be a non-starter for anyone not completely indifferent to global warming.

Unfortunately (but not unexpectedly) big coal has seized on the idea of producing gasoline from coal. Peabody Coal alone has estimated that switching to "liquid coal" would raise the value of company coal reserves almost ten-fold to $ 3.6 *trillion*[63]. *That is about $3 trillion extra that consumers would have to pay.* With this sort of money at stake, we can expect political donations to dominate the debate: There is every chance that appalling policies will be proposed, and quite possibly be adopted. The coal industry in general, and Peabody Coal in particular have greatly stepped up their lobbying efforts in the light of the potential pay-off from support for energy independence.

Peabody has hired Richard Gephart (Democrat and former House majority leader) to push a $3 million annual lobbying effort[64].

A successful global warming policy that eliminated the use of fossil fuels, would automatically lead to energy independence. (Even a partially successful policy would achieve energy independence). However, the relationship is intransitive. A successful energy independence policy could be implemented in a way that would lead to huge increase in AFCO2TA. Indeed, *it is exactly such policies that would be in the best interests of big coal.*

Co-sponsors of the current (2007) coal-to-liquid support legislation are listed in Table 6. They come from 12 states, illustrating how widespread are America's coal resources. Commenting on the corresponding 2006 House Bill, Kraig R. Naasz President and Chief Executive Officer of the National Mining Association (NMA) said, "America's accelerating dependence on imported foreign oil can be stopped in its tracks if Congress takes bold steps to foster the deployment of technologies for converting abundant domestic coal into ultra-clean fuels. 'The American-Made Energy Freedom Act,' (H.R. 5890), introduced today in the House, embraces this critical component of our overall strategy to cut America's energy import bill and to take greater control of our economic destiny"[65]. Fine, so long as you are not interested in global warming.

Table 6: Legislators who have Sponsored or Co-Sponsored
Coal-to-Liquid Support Bills*

Representatives		Senators	
Rick Boucher	(IL)	Christopher Bond (MO)	
Mike Doyle	(PA)	Jim Bunning	(KY)
Denny Hastert	(IL)	Michael Enzi	(WY)
Baron Hill	(IN)	Mary Landrieu	(LA)
Jim Matherson	(UT)	Richard Lugar	(IN)
Charles Pickering (MI)		Mel Martinez	(FL)
Mike Ross	(AK)	Lisa Murkowski	(AK)
John Shimkus	(IL)	Barack Obama[66]	(IL)
Ed Whitfield	(KY)	Mark Pryor	(AR)
		Craig Thomas	(WY)

* Senate: Coal-to-Liquid Fuel Energy Act of 2007 (S154)
* House: Coal Liquid Fuel Act (HR 2208)

Energy independence has also been used to justify subsidies to cellulosic and corn ethanol. These subsidies are less objectionable, since they do not actually increase AFCO2TA. However such subsidies are unwise in having Congress try to out-guess the market. If carbon is properly priced (i.e. taxed) then the various carbon-saving technologies are best left to find their own niches.

Terminating the use of fossil carbon will yield energy independence. Focusing on energy independence runs the risk of fostering investments that will have to be scrapped in the interests of controlling global warming.

Methane Hydrate: The carbon contained in ocean stored methane hydrate exceeds the carbon in all conventional fossil fuels combined. Release without sequestration would be disastrous. The potential exists for CO_2 to be sequestered as CO_2 hydrate as described in Boxes 3 and 4.

Box 3: Methane and CO2 Hydrates[67]:
Methane Extraction and Carbon Sequestration

In November 2000, somewhere off Canada's Vancouver Island, the commercial fishing vessel Ocean Selector brought to the ocean's surface an unusual "catch." The trawl net that had been dragged near the seafloor to capture fish recovered more than 1000 kilograms of methane hydrates from a depth of 800 meters.

Methane hydrates are ice-like solids in which water molecules form cages around molecules of methane, the chief component of natural gas. Methane hydrates are ubiquitous and found in ocean sediments—especially in continental margins—and the Arctic permafrost.

The accidental mining of methane hydrates by a fishing vessel caught the attention of Rod Judkins, director of ORNL's Fossil Energy Program. "This incident may suggest that some methane hydrates can be more easily recovered than we thought," he says. "Also, although these materials could have been broken off of outcroppings, it could indicate that hydrates are not necessarily covered with much sediment, which would imply that their formation does not require as much time as we have previously believed."

Judkins sees methane hydrates as the key to U.S. energy independence, which would give the nation energy security. "We must increase our primary energy sources to make us less dependent on foreign supplies of oil," he says. "One way to do this is to tap the abundant natural-gas supplies in methane hydrates, which offer us more energy than we have in our 1500-year-supply of coal. Estimates by the U.S. Geological Survey and others place reserves of methane in methane hydrates as high as 46×10^{15} m^3. This is an incredibly large potential energy resource, provided it can be safely and economically produced. Natural gas is a versatile fuel that can be used for generating electricity, heating homes, and fueling cars and trucks."

"In a research effort started with a seed money project and now continuing in a program funded by DOE's Office of Biological and Environmental Research, we found that intensely mixing water into liquid CO_2 within a specially designed injector produces a paste-like, cohesive mass that contains CO_2 hydrate," West says. "The presence of CO_2 hydrate, which is more dense than the seawater, caused this cohesive mass to be negatively buoyant, so it sank to the floor of the SPS vessel."

The picture that emerges is of a tight focus on national "energy independence" obscuring the globally far more important objective of stopping AFCO2TA, and active technology development by BP in cooperation with the DOE (Box 4) without any apparent thought for the likely impact on global warming. No doubt energy independence based on methane hydrate would be less bad than if it was based on coal, but that is little consolation. When BP adopted the motto "Beyond Petroleum", many of us thought they meant "Beyond Carbon", but sadly, apparently not. (See also Annex 9). *That DOE can be actively funding a search for new sources of carbon to release into the atmosphere boggles the mind!*

Annex 9, describes further progress in exploiting arctic hydrate reserves. In particular it notes that: *Heating offers a high production option for doing this (achieving energy independence) as the heat released from oxidation of a single methane molecule is enough to liberate over ten methane molecules from their hydrate state.* This suggests that methane hydrate could be highly unstable in the presence of oxygen.

No matter what developed countries achieve by way of reducing their reliance on coal, it is likely to be swamped by some 800 (dirty) coal-fired plants due to be constructed in China and India in the next five years. This is another "elephant in the middle of the room". It is bad enough that the Bush administration has done nothing constructive about domestic energy policy, but what can explain the administration's apparent lack of concern at the very rapid increase in the rate of AFCO2TA in the developing world? It is not reasonable to

Box 4: BP Drills Alaska North Slope Gas Hydrate Test Well to Assess Potential Energy Resource

BP Press Release date: 20 February 2007

Milne Point, Alaska (Feb. 19, 2007) -- BP Exploration (Alaska) Inc. successfully drilled a research well on the North Slope in partnership with the U.S. Department of Energy and the U.S. Geological Survey to collect samples and gather knowledge about gas hydrate, a potential long-term unconventional gas energy resource.

The stratigraphic test well enabled BP and the Department of Energy to gather core, log, reservoir performance and fluid data from an ice pad location at Milne Point. The drilling began Feb 3. Field teams began pulling hydrate core samples on Feb. 10. Extensive well logging and wireline formation testing was completed between Feb. 14-18.

"With this project, we have significantly increased our understanding of gas hydrate-bearing formations on the Alaska North Slope," said Scott Digert, BP resource manager and the project's technical adviser. "The results also illustrate the value of collaborative research," he said. This test well is part of the ongoing research partnership between BP and the Department of Energy, which began in 2002.

Known deposits of methane hydrate in Alaska and other parts of the world are enormous. However, the challenge is finding the technology to unlock the energy, to separate the natural gas from the solid gas-water-ice "clathrate" in which it occurs.

The DOE has identified gas hydrate as a research target and funded the estimated $4.6 million cost of drilling the Milne test well. BP contributed seismic data, staffing and program oversight. The on-site coring and data team included scientists from the USGS, DOE, Oregon State University and an observer from India's hydrate program.

Drilling crews and research team members collected about 430 feet of core samples. The cylindrical core segments, about 3 inches in diameter, were initially subsampled and analyzed on site due to the time-and temperature-dependent data requirements. They will be shipped to Anchorage for temporary storage before being distributed to gas hydrate researchers around the country. Subsequent data collection and analysis will continue for several months. A report of findings will be released thereafter.

seek a simple moratorium on coal generation plants in the developing world, but it might be possible to persuade and if necessary help them to move massively into nuclear power. On present projections, by 2012 these new coal fired plants will be adding almost 0.7 billion tons of carbon to the atmosphere each year. This is truly frightening.

(We return to this topic in Chapter 11).

Chapter 6:   Cap-and-Trade

We have seen what can be achieved by personal virtue, the limitations on the concept of carbon neutrality so long as carbon credits are limited only by the imagination of the vendor, and the long delay before we will even know if sequestering CO2 from FutureGen power plants (i.e. clean coal) is commercially feasible.

Regulation provides another approach, where polluters are given individual "caps" on the amount of emissions they are allowed to release. The proposed cap is often based on historic or established pollution levels (the big polluters get the big rewards). Regulation can be done in many ways. It can be targeted at the major polluters, leaving them to decide how to distribute their production, or by limiting the permits to industrial users of fossil fuels, via rationing related to past consumption levels. Regulation requires enforcement that involves having a cadre of inspectors and/or relying on industry to self-report.

The problems for such schemes are: How to set the caps or quotas? What to do if allocations prove to have been injudicious? How to ensure accurate reporting by industry (and indeed inspectors)? These problems are greatly reduced if polluters are allowed to trade "carbon credits" (or "pollution credits") amongst themselves, thus the name "cap-and-trade".

Chapter 4 discussed the limitations of carbon credits, if they are allowed to be created by supposed savings from sequestering bio-carbon, or claimed modified behavior. *For purposes of this chapter "carbon credits" refer only to credits generated by individual polluters who choose to pollute at levels below their assigned caps.*

It should also be remarked that amongst its other troubles Kyoto is fatally flawed by allowing countries to meet their emission reduction targets, by purchasing the imaginative types of carbon credit discussed in Chapter 4[68]. Even the EU, that should know better, seems to have fallen for this approach.[69]

Cap-and-trade (C&T) is a more flexible system than simple direct regulation. Under this system polluters who pollute less than their cap, can sell the balance of their allowance as "carbon credits" to polluters who need to exceed their cap. This increased flexibility reduces the difficulties from poor initial allocations, since if caps are set too low for some firms they can easily exceed the cap by buying carbon credits from polluters who are going to hold emissions below their cap.

C&T is often advocated as a way to limit the production of "greenhouse gasses". This involves the usual wooly thinking since, as discussed in Chapter 1, although CO_2 is a "greenhouse gas" and causes global warming, we do not want to eliminate it entirely, or we would freeze. Rather we want to limit adding *fossil* carbon dioxide to the atmosphere (AFCO2TA). Treating all CO_2 as equal is confusing, and easily leads to idea that AFCO2TA can be offset by sequestration of CO_2 in biomass: An inherently temporary sequestration. AFCO2TA should be controlled not by caps on CO_2 and methane emissions, but caps on the use of fossil carbon. It is also a mistake to try to control different greenhouse gasses with one cap. Different pollutants should have their own caps[70]. With different chemicals controlled by one cap, a credit (if valid) may represent a reduction in a totally different chemical to the one being released by the purchaser of the credit[71].

Note that under C&T pollution credits *should only generated by identifiable reductions in emissions by other polluters operating below their cap.* This is in marked contrast to the carbon credits discussed in Chapter 4 on carbon neutrality, where there is no physical limit on carbon credits, which tend to be limited only by the imagination of vendors.

We have seen that a strong argument for C&T is that under a regulatory scheme of "caps without trade", major problems are likely to be encountered between polluters as some individual caps are set too high, and some too low. Trade allows such "errors" to be corrected as those with too liberal a cap sell carbon credits to those with too tight a cap.

Even under C&T there is a problem as to where to set the caps? If the caps are set too high there will be ample (and therefore cheap) carbon credits, and little impact from the scheme. If the caps are set too low, then carbon credits will be scarce and expensive, and even "essential" needs may not be able to be met. Too low caps could lead to "cap induced blackouts" as demand simply exceeded the cap limited supply. This can be approached iteratively, with the first years caps set slightly on the generous side, allowing for tightening the following year.

Obviously, in an emergency polluters could be allowed to produce 110% or 120% of their cap[72].

To the extent that carbon credits are expensive the cost of purchasing carbon credits will be passed onto the consumer. An electric company forced to buy credits to meet customer demand for electricity, will have little choice but to pass on this extra cost to the consumer.

From one perspective, this is exactly what we want, since this higher price to the consumer should lead him/her to try to reduce or economize on electricity consumption. However it clearly leaves the consumer worse off.

But what happens to the seller of the carbon credit? The vendor can just treat it as miscellaneous income, leading to higher profits for the vendor. It is of course these extra profits from the sale of carbon credits that can be expected to motivate companies to cut back on their use of fossil fuel, in order to have carbon credit to sell.

Returning to the hypothetical electric company forced to buy carbon credits to meet consumer demand, and to raise the price of electricity to cover the cost of the credits. How will the electric company price the bulk of its electricity produced below its cap, and thus not requiring carbon credits to be bought? In most cases the company will raise the price of all its electricity to the same level as if it had been necessary to *buy* carbon credits[73]. All consumers will pay the higher price dictated by the cost of electricity produced above the cap. Again, there is an aspect of this that is desirable: all consumers will be encouraged to economize on electricity consumption.

But there is also a highly undesirable result. *The electric company (and other polluters) will get a windfall gain equivalent to its cap multiplied by the price of carbon credits.* The net result is higher prices for consumers and higher profits for polluters. This is not an intuitively desirable policy outcome, nor is it necessary as we will see in the next chapter.

A cap grants *the right to pollute up to the cap at no cost.* Why should anyone be given this right? Isn't the objective to discourage *all* pollution? *This is the fatal flaw of C&T: It rewards established polluters*: Hence the nickname Polluters Protection Program.

That this is not a hypothetical benefit to polluters is witnessed by the fact that some of the companies that originally supported the Climate Change Coalition[74], have reorganized as the United States Climate Action Partnership (USCAP). As the Climate Change Coalition they sought to dispute the existence of global warming, rewarding scientists and experts who would question the broad scientific consensus in supporting the existence of global warming. Starting in 1997 companies (led by BP) began to recognize that these doubts were untenable, and have subsequently formed USCAP with the Environmental Defense Fund[75] (EDF) and other environmental organizations. USCAP now says that global warming is real and serious, and sponsors C&T as the appropriate policy response: *Omitting to say that caps would give the sponsoring companies windfall gains, quite possibly reaching into the billions.*

Yes, caps could be tightened over time, until they fell to zero, but at enormous cost to consumers and enormous profit to polluters, in the mean time.

Moreover it makes a great deal of difference *who gets the caps.* There are three "pinch points" where ACO2 pollution could be capped, at the mine or well where the fossil carbon is produced, at the generating or chemical plant at which the fossil CO2 is released, or for the final consumer who ultimately causes the pollution, by his/her energy consumption.

Suppose that caps were placed on coal, oil and natural gas *production*, so that that the caps were assigned to mining, oil and natural gas companies. Suppose also that the caps were set at say 75% of production levels in 2007. What would happen? These companies, faced with demand well above the level at which they were allowed to produce, would have to raise coal, oil and gas prices so as to ration scarce supplies to their customers. Producing company's profits would rise markedly, energy prices to consumers would follow suit, and demand (consumption) would fall to level of available supplies. This is the magic of the market place, at work. Note however that this administrative arrangement would leave the producing companies (cap recipients) much better off and consumers much worse off. There might, of course be some small rationalization amongst producers, as small mining, oil or companies, decided it would be more profitable to go out of production and sell their production credits.

Suppose, on the other hand, that the caps were given to generating plants, and chemical companies that released fossil carbon as ACO_2. What would happen? Now the mining, oil and gas producing companies would be faced with a substantial drop in demand, and they would have to lower prices in their competition for customers. Rather than receiving a windfall gain, producing companies would be faced with a windfall loss. Smaller produces would likely simply go out of production: Again, the magic of the marketplace at work.

Meanwhile the electrical generating companies and energy suppliers would find that retail demand greatly exceeded their permitted production levels, leading them to raise electricity, petrol and natural gas prices, so as to rations their limited supplies amongst their customers. Not only would the price of their raw material fall, but the price of energy sold would rise, giving them a two-fold windfall gain.

As a third alternative suppose that consumers were given transferable energy rations that could be bought and sold between consumers. What would happen? Firstly there would likely be a *fall* in the price of electricity, oil and natural gas, as energy producers and supplies competed for the reduced level of sales. There would also be an active trade in the consumption permits/rations, as consumers with high energy needs bought permits from those with lower needs.

In December 2006 the British Environment Secretary, David Miliband, proposed rationing carbon use at the level of the individual consumer[76]. As set out, he envisaged using the card at the supermarket just like a credit card. This is probably overly ambitious, but it would be possible to start with a consumer energy ration for say household energy, gasoline and travel.

Looking on the web, David Miliband's idea seems to have fallen on stony ground. It may be worth reviving, since the implications for income distribution are quite different from industry based cap and trade. If we are to have a "war on warmth": Why not? We have "wars" on about everything else, poverty, drugs and terrorists. Surely some equality of sacrifice is a reasonable objective?

All of which leads us to perhaps the strongest argument against industry based C&T: *It is bad for democracy.*

Think about it for a moment: Allocation of caps to primary energy producers, rather than those who release ACO2, has huge (HUGE) revenue implications. As a result we could expect correspondingly huge political contributions aimed at influencing the design and administration of the C&T scheme. *Do we want our representatives subject to the sorts of temptation C&T would generate?*

It would be possible for the government to auction pollution caps. In this case the revenue would go to the government, and the result would be similar to a carbon tax (as discussed in the next chapter), with the exception that in an auction the government would set the total caps to be distributed, but with a tax they would set the price of pollution credits. Even an auction system runs the risk of underestimating demand at higher prices, leading to cap induced blackouts.

Chapter 7:   The Answer

If you replace the payroll tax with a tax on CO2, it would discourage the destruction of the planet's environment without increasing total taxes. Al Gore, interviewed by Rolling Stone, June 2007

Let's just remember the question for which an answer is required: *Given a decision by a nation, state, province or city to stop adding fossil carbon dioxide to the atmosphere (AFCO2TA): How can they do this at least cost/maximum benefit to the citizens or voters?*

That is, we have finessed the question as to how to get a government to make this decision, and limit ourselves to how to implement the decision at least cost or maximum benefit. Some brief thoughts on international collaboration on global warming are presented in Chapter 11.

Clearly the first step is to concentrate on *fossil* carbon (coal, oil, tar sands, natural gas and cement), and thus avoid the total intellectual confusion that comes from a blanket attack on "greenhouse gasses" or even generalized carbon dioxide. (Chapter 10 discusses "Other Greenhouse Gasses").

With the focus on *fossil* carbon, it is evident that planting trees, preventing methane emissions from land-fills, or changing light bulbs[77] (all useful in their own way) have no direct impact on AFCO2TA. The problem is to reduce (and eventually eliminate) AFCO2TA. *The way to stop AFCO2TA is to stop using fossil fuels: It really is as simple as that.*

Rather than "carbon credits", with the false implication that some offsetting action can be equated to using fossil fuels, we need to recognize that *"carbon credits" or "permits to use fossil fuels" are permits to pollute.* The only reason to issue such permits is that an immediate and complete ban on the use of any fossil fuel would cause very sever economic disruption.

If we replace the trade in carbon credits, used by C&T, by "pollution permits" issued by the nation, state, province or city aiming to reduce AFCO2TA, we can eliminate C&T's inherent problem that polluters pay no penalty for polluting up to their cap. Because they would have to buy "pollution permits" from the first ton of fossil-carbon used, this free ride problem would be eliminated, and *polluters would have an incentive not to pollute from the very first ton of fossil-carbon used.*

Moreover this ensures that the revenue generated by the sale of the "pollution permits" goes to the controlling authority, rather than to established polluters. This is widely misunderstood see Box 5.

Government (national, state or local) sold "carbon credits", "permits to pollute" or a "fossil carbon tax" are essentially the same thing. For a price, the purchaser is given permission to AFCO2TA, the government revenues are increased, and after a time the cost of the carbon credits/pollution permits/taxes will be passed onto the consumer, thus raising the cost of living, and being "highly unpopular politically" as Senator Boxer observed. The antidote to this unpopularity is return the tax revenue to consumers in the form of a direct "energy dividend". Administratively, the energy dividend could be returned monthly in equal amounts to all registered voters, (thus excluding from the benefit green card holders, tourists and illegal immigrants). This would have the incidental advantage of giving citizens an incentive to register to vote. We examine the scope for such an energy dividend below.

A fossil carbon tax would be extremely easy to collect.

For municipalities or states the gasoline tax could be collected at the pump. For electricity and natural gas, suppliers could be required to collect the tax on their monthly bill to consumers. Note that since electricity can be fossil-free or fossil-based, electrical companies would have to document whether they were supplying consumers with fossil-based electricity, and only these consumers would be taxed[78]. Coal used directly by industry would be a little

Box 5: Political Perceptions.

The San Francisco Chronicle (18, May, 2007) reports Senator Boxer as telling the National Press Club that she "ruled out a carbon tax, widely viewed by economists as an efficient and quick way to encourage energy conservation and reduce fossil fuel consumption, especially gasoline, by raising prices. For that same reason, it is highly unpopular politically."

"There's no support for it," Boxer said. Clinton attempted early in his first term to impose an energy tax, but was hammered by Republicans and the idea hasn't surfaced seriously in Congress since.

Boxer instead favors a "cap and trade" system modeled on the approach taken in California's new law and in Europe. Under such a system, the government sets overall emissions levels and develops a market in emissions, in which companies can earn credits by reducing greenhouse gas emissions, or buy credits from other companies that can do so more cheaply. Such a system was initially adopted by Bush's father's administration to curb acid rain pollutants from power plants. The idea was initially denounced but has since been widely embraced. While leveraging market forces, it has the political advantage of targeting industry, while hitting consumers only indirectly.

"At the end of the day, it does the same thing," Boxer said of a cap-and-trade system versus a carbon tax. "You put a price on carbon."

Comment: Clearly Senator Boxer has the right end of the stick in recognizing that *if you want to get people to use less carbon you need to raise the price of carbon*. However, she appears to believe that it is better that the extra revenue from higher prices go to polluters (the (private) vendors of carbon credits) than to the government; since "taxes" are always politically unpopular.

Why consumers should be happier to pay higher prices to the power company, than to the government is unclear.

> In the report, it appears that Senator Boxer is concerned about *any* carbon emissions, thus failing to focus on the true culprit *fossil-carbon* emissions.
>
> Furthermore, Senator Boxer has stopped half-way in her reasoning, since she has not addressed what government should do with the extra tax revenue. In particular she has not tied the extra tax revenue to a reduction in other taxes or direct repayment to consumers. Such a tie, would leave total tax revenue unchanged (be "revenue neutral"), give tax relief to those most in need of it and shift the tax burden to a "sin tax" on something we do not want.

more difficult to collect, since there are a wide variety of suppliers, and a company may switch suppliers from month to month, depending on the price offered. However, it should be possible to identify all companies selling coal (and the major purchasers) within the relevant jurisdiction.

A national carbon tax should be collected when oil or natural gas is pumped from the ground or imported; and for coal when it is mined. Higher prices would then work their way through the system. Cement should be taxed when first formulated.

The difference between C&T and a revenue neutral-carbon tax is stark, if the caps are allocated free of charge to polluters on the basis of past levels of pollution, then the revenues created by the caps go to polluters (the new owners of the caps), whereas the revenues created by a carbon tax go to the state. The two schemes can be made very similar, if caps are dispensed with, and polluters have to buy carbon credit at auction from the state. In fact if the quantity of carbon credits offered is just enough to yield an auction price equivalent to the tax rate, the two schemes are almost identical. The difference is that with an auction total carbon credits on offer is fixed, with a tax, the tax rate is fixed. Polluters needing additional credit can get them at any time by paying the tax.

Central governments have been slow to take effective action to slow global warming. This being the case, municipalities and states or provinces have initiated actions to slow the warming. The idea of an energy dividend is equally applicable at any level of government. Of course if the dividend was small it might be better to pay it annually than monthly, but the idea of taxing energy use, and returning the revenue to all relevant registered voters equally can be applied at any level.

Note that the whole thrust of the scheme is that taxes are collected in proportion to carbon use, but the dividend is returned irrespective of carbon use. Thus those who reduce or have low carbon use will benefit from the scheme on balance, while those with a carbon intensive life-style will be penalized.

Note also that there may be an incentive for forward looking municipalities and states to introduce the carbon tax/energy dividend, since if they can reduce carbon use in the jurisdiction, they stand to benefit when and if a national scheme is introduced.

Turning now to the federal (U.S.) level. Data for 2003 says that the US emitted 1,580,175,000 metric tons of fossil carbon[79] in 2003.

Annex 5 derives figures suggesting that if we wish to halve consumption of coal-based electricity then the following tax structure would be consistent, if consumers left their expenditure on coal-based electricity constant as price rose[80], (a doubling of electricity price thus halving consumption):

Summary: Impact of a $250.00 tax per m.ton of carbon

Fuel	Unit	Price	Tax	Sum	Tax/Price%
Coal*	m.ton	$ 35	$187	$222	534
Natural Gas	therm	$0.775	$0.41	$1.185	53
Crude Oil	gallon	$0.777	$0	$0	0

* Coal is only 75% carbon, $187 = 250*0.75$

Alternatively, if consumers were able to switch from coal-based electricity to fossil free, so that they could substitute up to half their coal-based electricity with fossil-free, the relevant price changes would be:

Summary: Impact of a $150.00 tax per m.ton of carbon

Fuel	Unit	Price	Tax	Tax/Price%
Coal	m.ton	$ 35	$113	222
Natural Gas	therm	$0.775	$1.02	32
Crude Oil	gallon	$0.777	$0.0	0

The zero tax on gasoline reflects the fact that gasoline is already taxed at about $0.42 per gallon, which is higher than the tax ($ 0.31 per gallon) required to yield $ 250 per ton of carbon.

However, there are other considerations that may well justify a higher tax, namely the heavy dependence on imported oil, and the evident easy savings by increased fuel efficiency and reduced use of the private car. *Accordingly "the answer" includes an additional tax of $0.58 on crude oil to bring the tax on gasoline to $1.00 a gallon.* Note that this is to some extent arbitrary, but reflects the widespread unease in the U.S. at being so dependent on imported oil.

Either way, these are very substantial tax rates that would generate a lot of revenue, but how much?

US Fossil Fuel Tax Base 2006.

Fossil Fuel	Units	Production	Imports	Total
Coal[81]	million short tons	1,164	36	1,196
Natural Gas[82]	billion cu.ft.	18,074	3,720	21,794
Crude Oil[83]	million barrels	1,890	3,677	5,567

Correction for Petrochemical Use

Fossil Fuel	Units	Total	Petro-chemical	Energy
Coal	m.tons	1,196	0	1,196
Natural Gas	b.cu.ft.	21,794	6,745	15,049
Crude Oil[84]	m.barrels	5,567	255	5,312

Proposed Fossil Fuel Tax 2006, ($250 per ton of carbon)
                    ($ 68 per ton of CO2)

Fossil Fuel	Units	Total	Conversion	Tax	$B
Coal	m.tons	1,196	1.00	187.50	224
Natural Gas	b.cu.ft.	15,049	0.0102@	0.41	63
Crude Oil*	m.barrels	5,312	42	0.58	129
Total $B					406

@ therms per cubic foot.
* 5,312(million barrels)*42(Gallons per barrel)*
    *0.58 (Tax as $/gallon) = $129 million tax income

With a approximately 200 million citizens 18 years and older, the $400 billion revenue would permit an annual energy dividend of $2,000, or $ 166 per month. Currently, only about 72% of citizens are registered to vote, so that initially the monthly dividend could be as much a $230. Hopefully, registration would be positively affected, and the dividend would accordingly decline.

These taxes apply to fossil carbon to be used for energy production, and thus AFCO2TA. Substantial amounts of natural gas and some oil are used in the plastics and chemical industries where the resulting product sequesters the carbon. So long as the product sequesters carbon essentially "for ever" the corresponding raw material should be tax exempt. Fossil fuels burnt for energy in the plastics and chemical industries should be taxed as for all other fossil fuels, only natural gas and oil used for chemical processing should be exempt. Biodegradable plastic should not, of course be exempt, since as the plastic degrades it AFCO2TA.

Gan and Smith[85] have estimated that a tax on only $25 per ton of CO_2 ($92 per ton of carbon) would be sufficient to make logging residues competitive with coal for electricity generation, and that dedicated poplar plantations would require a tax of $100 per ton of CO_2 ($ 367 per ton of carbon) to be competitive with coal.

The answer is thus to provide citizens (actually registered voters) a monthly energy dividend of from $166 to $230 (depending on proportions of citizens registered to vote) paid for by a carbon tax of $250 for coal and natural gas, and the equivalent of $1.00 per gallon on gasoline.

Important benefits are:

i) The tax is collected in proportion to use of fossil carbon, and

ii) The dividend is paid irrespective of carbon use, thus rewarding low fossil fuel users, and penalizing those with a fossil fuel-intensive life style.

Ancillary benefits include:

i) A substantial incentive to register to vote (although this implies no compulsion to actually vote), and

ii) Avoidance of the heavy political lobbying that could be expected if caps were given to individual companies. (Significant lobbying by energy producers against the whole scheme could, of course still be expected).

Subsidy for Sequestration? Chapter 1 mentioned that sodium hydroxide can be used to capture ACO2, despite the concentration in the atmosphere being only 0.04%. This is not yet a proven technology, and current cost estimates (about $400 per ton of carbon captured and sequestered) are excessively high. Logically, if there is a case for taxing people who AFCO2TA, there would seem to be a case for subsidizing people who remove *and sequester permanently* carbon from the atmosphere. Note however that current sequestration technology does not claim to reverse the burning of fossil fuels.

Burning fossil fuels takes sequestered carbon and adds CO_2 to the atmosphere current sequestration technology proposals would remove CO_2 from the atmosphere *and sequester it as CO_2*. There is no doubt about the stability of traditional fossil fuels in their natural state (although the stability of methane hydrate, a potential fuel, is in question). The long term stability of sequestered CO_2 remains to be demonstrated. This makes a strong case for subsidizing/funding research into ACO_2 capture and sequestration, but not a straight subsidy until we are clearer as to what is on offer. 3.67 tons of CO_2 have to be sequestered for every ton of carbon used.

While burning fossil fuel and (successful and permanent) sequestration have balancing effects on the carbon cycle (one adding carbon while the other removes it) they differ significantly. Undisturbed fossil fuel deposits can be expected to remain *in situ* for literally millions of years (they have already done so). The fate of sequestered CO_2 is less well known. It may prove to be as stable and storable as fossil fuel, but we will not know this for a few million years. Also fossil fuels are an energy source, whereas CO_2 is not: It is the byproduct of extracting the energy from fossil fuel. There is an element of danger, in having large stores of sequestered CO_2, lest they escape and warm the planet. In the longer term there could be advantages to having stored CO_2: If, for whatever reason the earth faced a new ice-age due to insufficient energy input from the sun, reservoirs of CO_2 could be activated to keep more of the incoming energy, and so avoid re-entering an ice-age.

Box 6: An Idea Whose Time Has Come

Letter to NYTimes 6/6/2007:

Mr. Friedman is correct in his advocacy of a gasoline tax to provide incentive for conservation and alternative fuels development. But the regressive nature of such a tax, which might cost an average driver $500 to $1,000 a year, would place an additional burden on lower-income individuals, and it would hardly slow down higher-income individuals in pursuit of high-power automobiles.

A solution for low- to middle-income individuals might be to let the gas tax offset another regressive assessment, like Social Security, basically having the government pay, say, the first $600 of Social Security assessment for lower-income taxpayers out of the revenue generated by the gasoline tax.

This would make the tax essentially revenue-neutral for lower-income people, but it would give them the incentive for added savings through conservation (car pooling, public transportation and so on).

The financial incentives to go green for upper-income individuals will have to be greater than the return on investment generated by a gas tax. This might mean adding a fairly stiff gas-guzzler tax, assessed yearly on new autos bought after the legislation is enacted that get less than, say, 35 miles per gallon.

James W. Pretz

Cincinnati, June 5, 2007.

The writer is chief executive of a consulting engineering firm.

While we are dangerously close to a tipping point, if not beyond one, it would seem sensible to encourage commercialization by offering a subsidy of up to $400 per ton, for up to a total of 1,000 tons/year of sequestered carbon. This could be bought using a Dutch auction (where the offer price is slowly raised until all required purchases have been made), thus encouraging the development of cheap technologies (always subject to specified technical levels of performance and reliability).

And Afterwards? Assuming this policy was adopted, and successful (i.e. we ceased to use fossil fuels, or subsidized CO2 sequestration left neutralized any fossil carbon releases), what would this new equilibrium look like? The first point to make is that the take from the carbon tax would decline as the use of fossil carbon declined. Initially this could be compensated for by higher tax rates on the remaining use of fossil carbon, however at some point tax take would decline, and indeed would be zero when the use of fossil carbon dropped to zero. The reader is right to ask: What then?

To maintain the tax base (be revenue neutral) it would be necessary to lower (and eventually eliminate) the energy dividend, while maintaining the high carbon tax (to prevent any reversion to cheaper, but polluting fuels). Consumers would be faced with (a) higher energy prices, (b) zero energy dividend but (c) eventual stabilization of the climate. It is not possible to estimate how much energy prices would have increased, but with plug-in hybrids, increased wind-farm efficiency, better constructed/insulated houses, etc., it is to be expected that it would be substantially less than it would be with use of current technologies.

Not only has the idea of a carbon tax been understood in some academic circles since 1992, but the idea of a revenue neutral tax is entering the public consciousness, see Box 6. This contribution is only concerned about taxing gasoline, but the idea generalizes very easily to all fossil fuels.

To repeat:

The answer is thus to provide citizens (actually registered voters) a monthly energy dividend of from $166 to $230 (depending on proportions of citizens registered to vote) paid for by a carbon tax of $250 for coal and natural gas, and equivalent of $1.00 per gallon on gasoline.

For some ancillary measures see Chapter 12.

Chapter 8:   Modifications

The last chapter ended with: **The answer is thus to provide citizens (actually registered voters) a monthly energy dividend of from $166 to $230 (depending on proportions of citizens registered to vote) paid for by a carbon tax of $250 for coal and natural gas, and the equivalent of $1.00 per gallon on gasoline.**

More correctly this should be described as *an* answer. There are a wide range of similar schemes that can be proposed, some based on a carbon tax, others on carbon caps, and still others on direct regulation.

Key issues are:

i) *Ease of administration.* Caps or taxes can be imposed when the fossil fuel is mined/pumped or imported, or they can be imposed at the point of use (power station, steel-works, gas pump, household fuel bill, etc.) In general it would seem that the fewer the collection/regulation points the simpler to administer the scheme. This argues in favor of setting caps or collecting taxes at the first point of extraction or importation.

Tying implementation to the almost infinite points of end-use presents an administrative (and political) nightmare. Administratively are we to rely on users self-reporting, or inspection? Do we want to have every furnace in every factory monitored? How to distinguish between fossil and fossil-free electricity at the point of use? A nightmare! Moreover, collection at the point of use invites political lobbying to obtain exemptions. Farmers, truckers, hospitals, mass-transit can all argue their special status and that pass-through of their higher fuel costs would be exceptionally inflationary. If the tax is collected before the end use is known, it is much harder for these lobbies to make their case.

One exception is where oil or natural gas is being used to make plastics or other products that will naturally sequester the carbon they contain. Better to tax everything, and refund where permanent sequestration can be demonstrated. In particular, taxation at source would (presumably) get around the international agreements that forbid taxation of aviation fuel. Ease of administration also argues for taxation rather than capping, although it is possible to envisage allocating caps to individual mines or oil-fields, and then allowing trading of these caps.

It is not impossible to cap at source, but it would clearly be cumbersome. *Capping at source would have major income implications for both energy companies and major polluters.* Limiting production of fossil fuels would lead to price rises, and windfall profits to the extractive energy companies. Capping at the point of use, gives the windfall profits to the using/polluting company. Where to cap, should lead to major disputes between extractive energy companies such as Exxon, and energy users such as electric utilities and Alcoa.

As David Miliband has suggested, it would also, conceptually, be possible to cap (ration) at the level of the individual consumer, and indeed would appear practical for major expenditures such as domestic energy use, gasoline and travel. Again, as pointed out earlier this too would have major income distribution implications. If billionaires and the unemployed had the same ration for fossil carbon use, it is likely that the rich would make huge payments to the poor, in order to get access to the carbon credits needed to support a jet-set life style.

Taking the above considerations into account, it is evident that a carbon tax would be much easier and fairer to administer than C&T, especially if collected at source.

ii) *Complete Coverage*. A tax (or cap) collected at the point of production (the mine or well) could conceivably cover all fossil carbon. It is difficult to see how attempts to collect taxes (or set caps) at the point of use could achieve complete coverage. Certain segments of the energy market, such as retail gasoline, electricity, and natural gas could be expected to achieve complete coverage at the point of use however exhaustive coverage of coal usage would likely be an administrative nightmare. For coal it is likely that the tax (cap or regulation) would be applied to all users in excess of some amount of tons per year. Thus letting small scale users escape.

iii) *Flexibility.* Initial tax or cap levels may be revealed to be too high or too low. If caps are set too high, there will be little reduction in AFCO2TA, if they are too tight, the prices generated by C&T may be unacceptably inflationary, or there may be "cap induced blackouts". If taxes are too low, there may be little economizing on fossil fuels, if taxes are set too high, they may feed through into too high levels of price inflation, or lead to economic stagnation or depression[86]. Cap induced blackouts are not something we want to contemplate. In theory, power companies could always buy extra carbon credits from the market however there can be no assurance that there will always be sellers. Caps could be relaxed in the event of a too high market price, but this is an incentive for power generators to be "caught short". On balance, it is probably easier to change tax rates (as can be done overnight) than to re-set caps.

iv) *Government Revenue.* How much revenue will be generated? Most discussion of C&T proposes that caps be given (free of charge) to established polluters, who could then trade. There is no necessity for a free distribution of caps, since the government could equally well charge, so much per ton of carbon, for caps, allowing companies to nominate the cap they want, up to some historically justified level, or sell caps at auction. Such a scheme would allow C&T to generate about as much income as a tax. Indeed if the government set the price of the cap, at the same level as a tax would have been set, the two schemes would come close to merging into one another.

v) *Whose Bull Gets Gored?* As discussed in the last chapter, the price changes needed to induce drastic behavioral changes involve serious amounts of money, quite possibly approaching half a trillion dollars, in the U.S. Who will pay this? Clearly the ultimate consumers of carbon produced services. But who will get it? That depends on the design of the scheme. If we have caps distributed without charge, then *the polluters can be expected to eventually benefit from the higher prices necessary to induce changed behavior.* In the author's view, this is entirely unacceptable. *A carbon tax ensures that the government gets the proceeds from higher prices,* although this same result can be obtained by C&T with a charge for cap allocations, or sale by auction. As discussed in (ii) above, it makes a huge difference to the revenue implications of a C&T scheme if (free) caps are given fossil fuel producers or users.

vi) *Revenue Neutrality.* If caps are distributed free of charge, there is no government revenue, so the scheme is "revenue neutral" in a degenerate sense: Consumers would pay billions more, and polluters would bank it. If either through a tax, or charge for caps, the government gets a (huge) revenue stream, there are many ways this could be used. For research, on public transport, you name it. However, it is integral to "the answer" that the extra revenue be returned to taxpayers in a progressive way, so that in aggregate they are no worse off. This is key to the "revenue neutral, carbon tax" mantra. The choice should not be between C&T and a carbon tax (as Barbara Boxer, see Box 5, implies) but rather between a "revenue neutral (charged for) C&T scheme", and a "revenue neutral carbon tax".

vii) *Phase In.* The fossil free world will be a very different world. There is a question as to how quickly we should try to enter it. Given the urgency of arresting global warming we should aim for the maximum feasible rate, consistent with avoiding major social or technical disruption. Different people will have different views as to how quickly this is, and in particular what is politically feasible. Given the seriousness of the problem there is everything to be said for "shock" treatment. At the very least policy makers and politicians *should be crystal clear that the objective is to dispense with the use of fossil fuels*. A carbon tax of $250 a ton was proposed in the last chapter, since this is a revenue neutral carbon tax, there does not seem to be a good argument for delay in its introduction, or even gradual introduction. While it would be possible to introduce the tax in say five annual increments of $50, this would (a) delay the beneficial effect of adjustment to the new price levels, and (b) even more importantly, give space for the Global Climate Coalition and USCAP to organize disruptive political opposition, such as lobbying/rental of key legislators. An advantage of a rapid and robust deployment is that it will give vested interests less time to organize. In any case, rate of implementation should not be a sticking point.

viii) *Magic of the Market Place.* Both approaches rely on the market to distribute price signals throughout the economy. The magic of the market place works in two ways. On the one hand it automatically accumulates costs, so that the cost of pump irrigation, artificial fertilizer, packaging, transport, freezer space and the like are all reflected in the price of an item in the supermarket. To the extent that a carbon tax affects these cost components, it will automatically be reflected in the product price. On the other hand if a cheaper way of doing things is discovered (rail versus truck transport) the market forces businesses to use it. This is because the lower cost gets reflected in the price of the product, and consumers buy what gives them the best value. High cost leads to higher prices, leads to poorer value, leads to loss of customers, leads to going out of business. George Mobiot has a fascinating account of talking to a supermarket manager about wasteful energy use in stores, citing several examples where energy was being used wastefully, but where it was "profitable to be wasteful". If the store was to be profitable, it had no option but to be wasteful of (cheap) energy[87]. Prices act both as a guide to action, and as a compulsion.

ix) *Income Distribution.* The magic of the marketplace depends on consumers being guided by price. This means that for many decisions the very rich would be unlikely to be influenced by a carbon tax. Perhaps in the choice as to whether to have one private plane or two[88], but not as to how often to fly the Atlantic, let alone what car to buy, or where to set the thermostat. Thus income distribution within the developed world is a relevant issue for global warming. Carbon rationing at the level of the individual would rapidly affect the lifestyle of the very rich. By the same token, income disparity between the developed world and developing world leads to economizing in very different ways. A developing world farmer may have to weigh how much rice to eat in order to afford shoes, where we in the developed world would almost always be able to have both. It is crucial to remember in policy discussions that although C&T and a revenue neutral-carbon tax can yield the same price/market incentives, the income distribution implications are likely to be very different.

x) *Regulation.* Some issues are most easily dealt with by regulation. Now that we know of *passivhaus* design standards, it would be more effective to regulate that all new construction and rehabilitation comply with these standards, than to hope that fuel prices alone would eventually lead to the same result. As remarked in the last paragraph the very rich are unlikely to be influenced in house design by cost, but regulation that requires technical standards can, in theory at least, be applied even to the very rich. There are always going to be people with so much money that price signals can be ignored. Regulation cannot be ignored (absent exceptional political clout). Fuel economy standards were very effective in producing more efficient cars. Regulation may be needed to force utilities to buy retail electricity as well as sell it, and so on. Regulation can, of course be used in addition to C&T or a revenue neutral carbon tax.

xi) *Regulatory Reform.* All regulations inhibiting the development or construction of fossil-free electrical generation should be reviewed and streamlined so as to facilitate new construction of such fossil-free plants, including nuclear.

xii) *Banning.* Regulation, in the extreme form of banning can also be appropriate. In the case of fluorocarbons, man-made greenhouse gasses with virtually no decay process and very high GWP (Global Warming Potential), banning is the appropriate policy. Currently developing countries are given a free ride in the use of fluorocarbons and chlorofluorocarbons. This makes no sense. Countries sophisticated enough to make such man-made chemicals, deserve no exception to a global ban. Clearly, there should be no new leases (by the private of public sector) for fossil fuel production. Although higher electricity prices will lead to lower demand, and abandonment of many planned fossil fueled power plants, it might be useful to simply ban construction of such plants in the absence of sequestration of the CO2 produced. The object of such a ban would be to send a clear signal to business, citizens and politicians that serious life-style changes will be needed to combat global warming.

xiii) *Drop Energy Subsidies*, including subsidies for fossil free energy production. This will be counter intuitive to some readers, for "surely we want to encourage fossil-free energy production?" The recommended action program gives very substantial encouragement to fossil free energy production *by doubling the cost of fossil based electricity*, together with removing regulatory obstacle to new fossil-free electricity production. This will certainly lead to substantial investment in new fossil-free generating capacity. We do not know which technologies will dominate, but we do know that (without subsidies) they will be competing on a level playing field. Any technology specific subsidy tends to divert investment away from other technologies that may be economically more efficient. If we want to provide even more encouragement to fossil-free energy production in general, then we should make a further increase in the carbon tax.

Quite apart from the economic efficiency argument, there is also a political argument. Subsidies are fickle. Given by one administration, they may be taken away by the next. This increases uncertainty for investors, and reluctance to invest, despite the subsidy. That is why it is of primordial importance that we establish a national consensus that **we intend to cease AFCO2TA.** With this assurance, investors can be fairly certain that there will be a big and increasing energy gap to be filled, and to invest accordingly. But there is another reason technology subsidies are to be discouraged: *They undermine the political process.* These subsidies need to be renewed (or at least protected from repeal) from time to time. As a result companies have an incentive to lobby and contribute to political campaigns in order assure the votes of influential representatives and to keep them in power. A subsidy measured in billions from the national treasury, is almost always accompanied by lobbying and political contributions in the millions that tip the electoral process in favor of incumbents, and lead these same incumbents to favor special interests over the national welfare. *Subsidies (and tax loopholes) are the feed-back that keeps the K-Street scandal going.*

xiv) *Sequestering.* The only sequestering that takes (at least for a while) carbon out of the cycle, is sequestering of CO2, or charcoal. There are examples where CO2 sequestration seems to be working (see Box 2). It has been argued that for administrative simplicity it would be best to collect the tax, or set the caps at the mine, well or point of import. Once the technology is proven, power plants sequestering CO2 could then be paid a subsidy per ton of carbon sequestered. (Because of the income transfer issue, caps should be charged for).

xv) *Documentation.* Although the carbon tax and energy dividend are designed to be revenue neutral, they can never be cost-neutral to each and every tax-payer. There are going to be individuals who are severely disadvantaged by the new policy, and even classes of people badly affected. Such cases will surely be found and quickly documented and publicized by reactionary groups such as USCAP. It is thus important that introduction of the tax be accompanied by a program of social surveys to establish the impact of the tax: Both to allow heuristic improvement of the tax, and to defuse atypical individual horror stories.

xvi) *Subsidy Repeal.* All explicit and implicit subsidies for fossil fuel production or consumption should be terminated immediately, including under-priced leases and non-collection of royalties owed to the government[89]. On the consumption side programs that subsidize fossil fuels (such as winter fuel subsidies to the poor) should be replaced by income subsidies unrelated to fuel usage. *It makes no sense to subsidize global warming!*

Chapter 9:   Technology⁹⁰

We can already see that several key technological system required for a fossil-free economy will be markedly different from the technologies developed in the face of plentiful (almost free) fossil fuels. In particular the electrical grid needs to change, cars need to go hybrid and rechargeable, and air travel will need to be greatly curtailed. In each case, there is a chicken and egg problem. Wind-farms will lose much of their potential value if we do not have a national direct current grid, but there is no point in building such a grid, absent wind and solar power generation to use it. Effective driving range on electricity from plug-in hybrids would be doubled if all parking spaces were routinely equipped with electrical sockets, but why provide this infrastructure in the absence of plug-in hybrids? And so on.

There is a key role for government in ensuring that the enabling support technologies be put in place. This does not mean that government has to make the investments (although in some cases this may be cost effective), but it does need to ensure that *someone* is going to make the investments. Investments which, as mentioned earlier, could well spark a long-term boom.

The Grid: The current electrical grid serves a mix of power stations with nuclear (always on) carrying the base load, coal and hydro (mostly on) adding mid-range capacity, and natural gas (mostly off) to provide peak load. *The important characteristic of this legacy system is that all power sources can be switched on and off as needed.*

Hospitals, computer centers, airports, emergency services, etc. need power 24/365 and they typically have their own stand-alone back-up systems that can be quickly brought into play in the event of a black-out. In total this provides substantial additional generating capacity.

Electrical power cannot be stored as electrons (within the grid), "use it or lose it" is the operating rule together with "if demand exceeds supply, no one gets power". The system is a little bit forgiving, as voltage fluctuations can absorb minimal imbalances for short periods.

Our fossil free future will increasingly be reliant on power sources (wind, waves and solar) that switch themselves on and off: That produce when they feel like it. This requires a different (high voltage, direct current (DC)) grid: One that can transfer power over long distances with minimal transmission losses[91]. We will need this long distance power transfer in order to source power from where it is available. The wider the geographical reach of the grid the more likely it is that it will be connected to active generators.

The grid will also need to be connected to electrical storage. Always difficult, the most effective electrical storage currently is pumped storage, by which electricity to be stored is used to pump water into a high altitude lake or dam. When the electricity is needed, water is released to drive turbines, and is collected in a lower level lake or dam. Note that such pumped storage can be used to store power from nuclear generators when demand is low. Domestic oil storage heaters can also be used to transfer heat (electricity use) from periods of low cost electricity, to higher cost times.

Quite apart from fluctuations in supply, there are also seasonal and diurnal fluctuations in demand. It is to meet these fairly predictable demands that the legacy (AC) grid connects base load, mid-range, and peak load generators. In summer air-conditioning demand typically peaks mid-day to early afternoon. Fortunately this coincides with peak production from photo-voltaic cells.

An AC (alternating current) grid is cheaper to construct than HVDC (high voltage direct current), although the cost of HVDC is falling fast. Transmission losses per mile are higher for AC than HVDC, so that currently HVDC transmission is cheaper beyond 650 kilometers.

The legacy AC grid system, operates by adjusting supply to demand, and can switch on or off the closest peak generating capacity as needed. This allows it to keep transmission distances (and hence losses) reasonable.

For wind, solar and wave power the grid needs to be able to accept power when available, and transfer it to where it is needed (which may be over very long distances). This dictates a new HVDC grid backbone, interfacing locally as needed with the legacy grid. Since supply may exceed demand, the new grid will need to be connected to pumped storage sites that allow mechanical storage of excess electricity. This is a technological innovation needed to ensure that generating capacity can be expanded effectively to respond to the new price signals.

Managing Demand: As already noted the legacy grid adjusts supply to demand. The new HVDC grid will enable available power to be shifted over long distances to where it is most urgently needed. However, this is only half the story. *We also need innovation in demand management.*

Clearly some domestic uses of electricity are more important than others. A consumer might rank her electrical needs in descending order such as:

i) computer and phone

ii) central heating if house under 36 degrees Fahrenheit (to avoid pipes bursting)

iii) Five lights and refrigerator/freezer, recharge the car

iv) Air-conditioning if over 82 degrees Fahrenheit

v) Stove, balance of lights and most power-plugs

vi) All systems.

With this ranking she could then set maximum prices she was willing to pay for each demand segment. This coupled with real-time electricity pricing by the grid, would allow demand to be reduced (by raising the real-time price) as the grid came under increasing pressure.

Any such dynamic demand management will require household electronics able to respond to real-time price signals, and able to reflect the consumers willingness/ability to pay.

In conditions short of a blackout, the stand-by capacity of hospitals and emergency services could be switched on to feed into the grid. And as we move to more sophisticated hybrid-cars, we may get to the point where the house can be plugged into the car, to keep essential Tranch #1 services going.

Plug-In Hybrids: Plug-in hybrids will allow all the advantages of hybrid, together with the capacity to plug into household current, so as to be fully charged each morning[92]. These cars are currently expected to be able to drive up to 30 miles on a fully charged battery (i.e. before the engine needed to be turned on), and at a cost of 3 cents a mile for electricity, (even with the proposed doubling of the cost of electricity, this would still be only 6 cents) versus 12 cents a mile for gasoline. If parking lots were routinely provided with a charging plug, this 30 mile radius could in many cases be expanded to 60 miles. Charging is slow, but if the driver is going to spend 8 hours in the office anyway, she could well find her car fully charged for the return commute. As soccer mums know, a large number of excursions involve quite short distances. Some Canadian cities already provide plugs to allow parked vehicle to warm their engines in winter. If the electricity was fossil-free, then the first 30 miles for plug-in hybrids would be cheap and fossil free.

Compressed Air Technology (CAT): The air-car is a revolutionary light weight vehicle designed to run on compressed air. Moteur Development International (MDI) was formed in 1991, and is headquartered in Luxembourg. It has developed a car design that can to about 250 miles at 30 mph, or 125 mile at 68 mph on a single charge of compressed air. From a commercial station it can be recharged in about two minute (at a cost of about $2.50 per charge), or with a home compressor in about four hours. About 6,000 "MiniCat" diminutive vehicles are expected to be sold in France in 2008, and Tata Motors is planning to produce an Indian version of the car. A MultiCat 8-cyclinder version is under development for public transportation. The current designs achieve their relatively good range and performance by using an extremely light weight design that would probably not meet American safety standards. However, it may eventually prove possible to design a model to meet American safety requirements[93].

Ethanol: There is no doubt as to the technical feasibility of producing bio-ethanol or bio-diesel. The problem is giving the market the right price signals. Currently bio-ethanol is doubly protected, firstly by a 54¢ tariff on imported ethanol, and secondly by a generous 51¢-per-gallon subsidy blenders get from the government[94].

Professors Pimentel and Patzek of the University of Minnesota have estimated that ethanol from corn produces 25% more energy than is consumed in growing, processing and shipping. This means that if ethanol was used in the production of ethanol, five gallons of ethanol would have to be produced (attracting a $2.55 subsidy) to have one gallon to sell.

The National Environmental Trust says that vehicles powered by ethanol get 20 to 30 percent fewer miles per gallon than they do with gasoline.

It appears highly unlikely that if the blending subsidy and tariff were removed corn based ethanol would be competitive with sugar cane bases ethanol from Brazil. It is doubtful if even writing down recent investments in ethanol production plants in the corn-belt to zero, would allow corn-ethanol to be competitive. Bio-diesel should be no problem, and eventually the bugs may be worked out of the Iotech and Tigney processes for using waste biomass (corn stover, wheat straw, trash wood and the like) to make ethanol. However, the heavy push to promote corn based ethanol, looks like another example of government promoting the wrong technology.

High Speed Rail Travel: Obviously, long-distance air-travel is going to be extremely difficult to replace. However for trips of less than 1,000 miles high speed trains promise to be reasonably competitive, especially if scheduled over-night with sleeper cars for longer distances. Security checks and flight delays dominate actual travel time in making comparisons. Europe is fast developing a high-speed train network, with much of it operating at 200 mile per hour, and with a quarter to a tenth of the carbon dioxide of a plane[95]. To date, with the alternative of cheap and frequent air travel available, America has made no serious effort to emulate the fastest of the European high-speed trains.   A serious effort to achieve at least European standards of speed and reliability is needed. Ideally, these trains would be coordinated with bus transport to surrounding cities. And all train tracks should be electrified.

Hydrogen Economy[96]: We need to give up on hydrogen, it is a non-starter. In 2007, the Bush administration requested $196 million (out of a total energy research budget of $1.18 billion) for hydrogen, thus depriving technologies of real promise. It is Iraq all over again. The basic problem is that hydrogen has to be made before it can be used. Two technologies are available, stripping hydrogen from fossil fuels thus AFCO2TA if the carbon is not sequestered, or by electrolysis which would be a major waste of fossil free power. Not only is hydrogen dirty or wasteful to make, but making it available at gas stations would require a $500 billion investment, and no on-car storage technology exists that would give drivers an acceptable range, even if they could fill-up. The administration's advocacy of the hydrogen economy is a purely political device intended to give the impression of doing something about global warming without actually exploiting any of the immediately available technologies. We should not be fooled.

Collection: Klaus Lackner of Columbia University has developed a "stand-alone" CO_2 collector that uses sodium hydroxide to fix CO_2 from the atmosphere (even though the concentration is only 0.04 percent of the atmosphere). Given a substantial wind, CO_2 can be fixed even though you have to have 250 times the air-flow over the collecting surface to collect one volume. After collection the sodium hydroxide is regenerated by electro-dialysis that yields a pure stream of CO_2. This can be sequestered in geological formations as discussed in Chapter 5, or it could be mixed with magnesium or calcium-bearing minerals to form a carbonates and be put away safely and permanently. The important feature of this approach is that is permits an active program to reduce ACO_2 concentrations. Current cost estimates are about $400 per ton of carbon removed.

Collection: Still at the early experimental stage, several approaches are being explored to use the CO_2-rich exhaust from power stations to grow algae, thus capturing the carbon by photosynthesis. The algae could either be fed back into the power station, or used to make bio-ethanol. Either way it should lead to the fossil carbon being reused and giving a much higher energy generation per ton of fossil carbon. However absent a 100% efficient closed-cycle system a net input of fossil carbon would still be required[97].

Sequestration: Chapter 5 describes sequestration of carbon dioxide in geological formations and possibly as CO_2 hydrate in the deep ocean.

Solar Power: In addition to the low-tech solar water heaters seen on residential roofs, large-scale solar power generation systems are being developed, where mirrors (in troughs, parabolas, or directed to a central tower) automatically focus the sun on to power collectors that heat, water, oil or salt, to high temperatures, that are then used to generate electricity. A CEC (California Energy Commission) study shows that even with existing tax credits, a solar thermal electric plant pays about 1.7 times more in federal, state, and local taxes than an equivalent natural gas combined cycle plant. If the plants paid the same level of taxes, their cost of electricity would be roughly the same. Clearly this tax anomaly should be removed.

Geo-Engineering: The heating induced by higher ACO_2 could be compensated for by a quite modest drop in the amount of the sun's energy received by earth. This has led to a number of proposals to block or reflect sunlight on a global scale to achieve the needed reduction. None of these have yet gone beyond academic proposals.

Flying Wind-Farms: Terrestrial wind-farms are now almost a "conventional technology", opposed by some on scenic grounds, and subject to whether the wind is blowing. A proposal has recently been put forward to harvest wind from the jet-stream (six mile up) that are both stronger and more consistent than terrestrial wind. Flying generators look like a cross between a kite and a helicopter, with four rotors at the corners of an H-shaped frame, tied to the ground by an aluminum cable. When the wind blows (most of the time) the rotors both keep the structure flying and turn generators that send electricity to the ground via the aluminum cable. If the wind drops, the generators can be reversed to act as electric-engines, thus turning the rotors to keep the structure aloft[98].

Hydro-cooling: Toronto is drawing on the cold water of Lake Ontario, to provide air-conditioning cooling. Water is pumped from 3 miles into the lake and 83 meters deep to a heat exchanger (with the cool being transferred to tower-block air conditioning systems) and then purified for drinking water. At 83 meters and below water is at a constant 4o C (when water is at its densest), thus providing the needed cool[99]. The necessary conditions for this technology are a large metropolitan centre adjacent to a large deep and cold lake. Stockholm has used this approach using sea water, but Chicago was found to be unsuitable, since Lake Michigan is insufficiently deep around the city.

Other Technologies: New technologies are announced almost daily. It is impossible to offer a complete menu of energy alternatives. To find out which technologies are most cost effective, a level playing field on which they can compete is needed. This argues for removing technology specific subsidies, imposing a tax on carbon and subsidy on sequestration, and letting the market do the hard Darwinian work of sorting out the "fittest" systems, and the niches in which they are competitive.

Dispensing with fossil fuels will involve massive capital write-offs and massive investments in new capacity. Properly handled, the next three decades should be a period of economic boom. Obviously there are important choices as to the role of the public and private sector in these developments[100]. As mentioned repeatedly, it is essential that there be a clear statement of policy direction, to guide these write-offs and investments.

Chapter 10: Other Greenhouse Gasses

In addition to carbon dioxide and methane that are naturally occurring gasses within the carbon cycle, other greenhouse gasses include Nitrous Oxide (N02) and Nitrogen Oxide (NO), Ozone (O3), and Chlorofluorocarbons.

Nitrogenous gasses: Nitrous Oxide and Nitrogen Oxide (collectively NOx) contribute to the nitrogen cycle, whereby bacteria in the root nodules of legumes, "fix" atmospheric nitrogen and supply it to the plant. When the plant dies and rots, the nitrogen is restored to the atmosphere. This is the basic natural nitrogen cycle. Nitrogen itself is not a greenhouse gas: It does not contribute to global warming. A very little of the nitrogen released when plants rot, or through bacterial action is released as Nitrous Oxide. This is a powerful greenhouse gas (about 300 times as powerful as CO2) and capable of remaining in the atmosphere for as much a 100 years. Fortunately it occurs in very small volumes (0.3 ppm, versus 380 ppm for CO2).

For almost a century man has been interfering with the cycle, by using natural gas and nitrogen (from the atmosphere) to create anhydrous ammonia gas, by the Claude-Haber process. This is applied directly to the soil or converted to urea or ammonium nitrate for fertilizer. When the fertilizer is applied some nitrogen escapes directly into the atmosphere, and the balance is used by plants, returning to the atmosphere as nitrogen when the plant dies, rots or is eaten. Nitrogen represents about 80 percent of the atmosphere and does not affect global warming, so its build-up, if any[101], is of no concern. One could say that in manufacturing nitrogenous fertilizers, we are "accelerating" the nitrogen cycle, with only a slight effect on releases of nitrous oxide.

A high tax on natural gas would raise the price of nitrogen fertilizers. Other energy sources together with a hydrogen source can be used in place of the Claude-Haber process.

Nitrous oxide is also produced by cars and trucks, burning coal and by the production of acidic chemicals. However net additions to the nitrogen cycle are very small, and will be smaller as the use of fossil fuel for transportation is eliminated.

Ozone: Ozone (03) is a powerful, but short lived (just a few days) greenhouse gas. It is not released directly by fossil fuels, or other human activity, but is the result of oxygen combining chemically with nitrous oxide or nitrogen oxide in the presence of sunlight. The nitrogen oxide gases are released from burning gasoline or coal. Ozone concentration varies day to day, end even hour to hour, but is seldom above 0.03 ppm (versus 380 ppm for CO2). Elimination of fossil fuels will largely eliminate global warming from ozone.

Industrial Gasses: Come in two forms, as CO2 emissions from limestone and energy used in the manufacture of cement, and as fluorocarbons used for refrigeration.

Cement: Cement production accounts for more than 1.6 billion tons of CO2 or over 8% of total CO2 emissions from all human activities[102]. Manufacture one ton of cement releases 1.25 tons of C02: 0.75 tons from energy use, and 0.50 from calcining limestone. The CO2 from energy would be caught by a tax on fossil fuels, however we would need to also tax limestone used for cement.

The coliseum, our great cathedrals and roman aqueducts remind us that major public works can be built without concrete. However, dispensing with cement will demand a revolution in architecture and in the construction of large projects. Note that the advantage of a phased increase in fossil carbon taxes, as the tax rises masonry, steel and stone will be substituted for cement where this can be done at reasonable cost, while concrete will continue to be used for jobs where substitutes were not readily available. As alternative technologies are developed, and as taxes continue to rise, concrete will eventually be phased out.

Chlorofluorocarbons: Man made chemicals are another story. Chlorofluorocarbons (CFCs) were first introduced in the 1920s. They were cheap and used as coolants in air conditioners and refrigerators, propellants for aerosol sprays, and as agents used to produce plastic foam. In the 1970s, scientists reported that CFCs were rising high into the atmosphere and destroying the ozone layer[103]. CFCs were banned in 1995s under the Montreal protocol. They were replaced by hydrofluorocarbons (HCFCs) and perfluorinated compounds (PFCs). While the new compounds do not react with the ozone layer, HCFCs and PFCs were found to be *potent greenhouse agents.* They also were discovered to be very long-lived, making their accumulation in the atmosphere hard to reverse. New substitutes for these substitutes are being developed. A related compound, sulfur hexafluoride (SF_6), used in the insulation of electrical transmission systems, is another greenhouse gas. It has been rated as the most powerful greenhouse gas ever released into the atmosphere.

Under the Montreal Protocol developed countries committed themselves to phasing out CFC's, and to providing financial assistance to developing countries (notably China, India, Venezuela, Argentina, Mexico, Romania and North Korea) to phase out their use of CFCs, usually by substituting HCFCs. This has beneficial effects on the ozone layer, but an impact on global warming remains.

The phasing out of CFC's[104] seems destined to eventually restore the ozone layer. CFCs also contribute to global warming, as do HCFCs and PFCs. While CFCs, HCFCs and PFCs have Global Warming Potentials (GWPs) several thousand times as high as CO2, HCFCs and PFCs generally have shorter estimated atmospheric lifetimes, and lower GWPs then the CFCs they replace[105]. The next step will be to replace HCFCs and PFCs.

Unlike carbon and nitrogen there is no natural cycle for fluorocarbons, that are several thousand times more powerful greenhouse gasses than CO2[106], and in some cases these persist for decades, centuries or millennia in the atmosphere. Clearly the objective with these industrial gasses, as for fossil-carbon, should be to bring emissions to zero, that is to say *to cease using them.*

This could again be achieved by a "revenue-neutral fluorocarbon tax". Faced with a 100% (or higher) tax on fluorocarbons, manufacturers would quickly find ways to use ammonia, hydrocarbons, and (bio)-CO2.

This might be a case where direct regulation/prohibition of use would be appropriate. A country sophisticated enough to be using fluorocarbons, cannot plausibly claim to be "under-developed" at least in this portion of the manufacturing sector. A hiccup in manufacture, and higher prices once the alternative technologies can be mass-produced, would be a small price to pay for eliminating these dangerous man-made chemicals. The World Trade Organization (WTO) provides one possible route to enforcing a ban. The WTO already rules on whether a manufacturing technology qualifies for the protection of WTO rules in international trade. It would be but a small step to have the WTO also rule on the permissibility of technologies used for purely domestic purposes, as in the case of greenhouse gasses this "domestic" activity in fact affects the viability of nations world wide.

Chapter 11: International Cooperation

This book is clearly addressed to development of national or local strategies for combating global warming. However, as such strategies begin to emerge, it becomes increasingly urgent to deal with "the elephant in the middle of the room", namely the need for nations to work together to stop global warming. China and India alone are expected to build 800 new (and dirty) coal-fired power plants by 2012 (i.e. in the next five years) that will emit about 1.15 billion tons of carbon per year, this alone will increase the rate of AFCO2TA by 11 percent. That is about the total increase built into IPCC scenarios, implying that at least for the next five years, the IPCC models are likely to under-estimate the rate of global warming. The U.S. has over 150 power stations at some point in the planning/ construction cycle.

An alien visiting earth, would find it impossible to understand how having global problems, we still have no global government. Be that as it may, action on global warming cannot await global constitutional reform.

As discussed in Chapter 13, the IPCC scenarios are already being overtaken by events. China overtook the United States as the worlds leading polluting nation in 2006. As Dr. Fatih Birol of IEA said "within 25 years China's CO2 emissions will be double the CO2 emissions which will come from all the OECD countries put together - the whole US, plus Canada, Europe, Japan, Australia, and New Zealand. ...... Without China playing a significant role, all the efforts of every other country will make little sense. It is terribly important."

Because it is such a large economy, if the U.S. eliminated fossil carbon emissions this would make a serious (16%) impact on global emissions (at least until China and India ramp up further). However, this still leaves the other 84% of global emissions.

The President and many in the Senate have been playing "you first". They are unwilling to take action unless at least China and India commit to some level of restraint, and obviously China and India are unwilling to cut back their use of fossil fuels if America does not. This is a fine, righteous (not to say childish), recipe for deadlock. Think how other countries would react if America was able to show that it had cut emissions by 50%, and was well on the way to bringing them to zero. We would have demonstrated technologies to share with other countries, and the standing to say: It can be done.

What is more, with a nucleus of low polluting countries, it would not be long before pressure would build to exclude countries from international trade agreements that did not have proactive programs to reduce pollution. It is almost suicidal (or better ecocidal) to buy products, the production of which pollutes our atmosphere. The case for some sanctions on blatant and irresponsible polluters is overwhelming …….. once the feasibility of massive emission cuts has been demonstrated.

A major difference between Montreal and Kyoto was that in Montreal America played a constructive role. In Kyoto it played an uninterruptedly cynical and obstructionist role[107]. During negotiations the Clinton-Gore administration worked to (a) avoid enforceable commitments to reduce emissions, and (b) to minimize the commitment levels, threatening not to participate if American conditions were not adopted. Then having weakened the treaty to the maximum extent possible, America withdrew. Moreover, American private sector representatives from the Global Climate Coalition (aka the Carbon Club) also worked hand in glove with Saudi Arabia and Kuwait national negotiators to emasculate the treaty. Kyoto would be a much better treaty had the U.S. said from the start that it would not participate.

This chapter was consciously headed "International Cooperation" rather than "International Agreements", since what we want is freely given cooperation, rather than grudging "agreement". The way in which countries approach working together on global warming will very largely determine the success of their efforts. Box 7 describes an interesting private initiative that will contribute significantly to what Kyoto is designed to achieve. The initiative is interesting because of the positive and cooperative spirit that it illustrates.

Box 7: Global Coalition to Make Buildings Energy-Efficient[108]

This article reports on an agreement sponsored by the William J. Clinton Foundation, that brings major banks (contributing $ 1 billion each) together to provide loans to cities and private owners to retrofit existing buildings with appliances, upgraded heating, cooling and insulation.

The first targets for lending will be a range of large cities from B to T: Bangkok, Berlin, Chicago, Houston, Johannesburg, Karachi, London, Melbourne, Mexico City, Mumbai (formerly Bombay), New York, Rome, Sao Paulo, Seoul, Tokyo and Toronto.

This retro-fitting is expected to cut energy costs by 20 to 50 percent, and enable the loans to be repaid from these savings.

Four things are notable about this initiative:

- It will be making significant reductions in AFCO2TA using current technology. (No need to wait for the never-never promise of a hydrogen economy).

- It represents voluntary international cooperation, without a formal international agreement.

- It treats developed and developing countries equally.

- It should prompt city administrations to revue whether they should be more actively encouraging energy conservation measures.

As such, it illustrates that Kyoto type agreements are not the only way forward.

While it is true that developed countries have contributed much more to existing ACO2 levels than the developing countries, it is also true that rapidly developing countries have an urgent need to move quickly to less polluting technologies. The Independent on Sunday (7/8/2007) reported that China has five of the ten most polluted cities in the world; acid rain is falling on one-third of the country; half of the water in its seven largest rivers is badly contaminated and a quarter of China's citizens lack access to clean drinking water. Similarly the NYTimes reports that the Chinese wanted to remove from a joint study with the World Bank an estimate that 750,000 people die prematurely in China because of air and water pollution.

Thus while developing countries have less responsibility for the rising levels of ACO2 than developed countries, they may have even more incentive to do something about it.

If we could get agreement that the objective is to eliminate AFCO2TA, not to reduce the rate of AFCO2TA *but to eliminate it*, this would change the whole ethos of international collaboration. No longer would countries be seeking arguments as to why it would be too costly for them to reduce AFCO2TA, to be replaced by a focus on "how do we do this at least cost?" and "how can you help me (I help you) to achieve the goal?" Somehow we have to change the focus from "the *costs* of eliminating global warming" to "the *benefits* of eliminating global warming".

The long term goal should be to have *an international ban on the use of fossil-carbon for energy production.* In the mean time our focus needs to be on what policies and technologies work. Hopefully, when the first country puts in place a revenue neutral carbon tax, the results will be such that other countries see the advantage of moving to a "sin" tax; as countries move to adopt *passivhaus* specifications for new construction, others will follow; and so on. It is likely that much more can be achieved by collaboration than by confrontation.

Collaboration will need to be supported by an ongoing coordinating agency. A number of candidate agencies already exist:

i)   The United Nations has been helpful in sponsoring the IPCC (International Panel on Climate Change) and international environmental gatherings, but its modus operendi is not well suited to a continuing and routine involvement. It is too riven with blocks, and confrontational practices.

ii) The World Bank has no authority for dealing with developed countries, and the IMF (International Monetary Fund) does not have the necessary technological expertise.

iii) Strangely the World Trade Organization (WTO) may have some relevant expertise. The WTO mandate is to establish rules for "fair trade" amongst the membership (i.e. all major trading nations, and most small ones). This requires it to consider when is a subsidy a subsidy? What if any subsidies are permissible? When "health regulations" are actually being used to protect domestic industry? What labor practices are "fair"? And so on[109]. Most importantly it has an established dispute resolution procedure, heavily biased towards agreement between the concerned parties (countries) but with a clearly defined procedure and timetable if the concerned parties cannot reach agreement, and even provision for one level of appeal.

iv) The International Energy Agency (IEA) of the OECD (Organization for Cooperation and Development) is active in all aspects of energy, and provides global statistics on many dimensions of energy production, trade and consumption. Membership is currently limited to OECD countries. It would seem to have the breadth of view and capacity to act as a secretariat for international collaboration aimed at eliminating AFCO2TA.

Hopefully it will prove possible to embarrass countries into compliance, rather than to force them. International studies of the failure of the EPA to enforce its own regulations and consequent pollution; international documentation of the way the Bush administration has moved to weaken EPA regulation, or to muzzle public scientific reporting of the expected environmental damage from global warming, and so on, might credibly embarrass even the Bush administration into constructive action, and go a long way towards filling the vacuum created by poor quality of mainstream media reporting on environmental problems.

However, even more effective than shaming recalcitrant countries into action, would be a flood of success stories, as to how countries were cutting back on AFCO2TA, and policies and investments that work.

A recent Newsweek article[110] advocated a domestic carbon tax to discourage AFCO2TA, with the proceeds to be used to help developing countries to move away from coal to cleaner (and more expensive) energy source. At the very least, there would seem to be a strong case for consolidating the limited amount of foreign aid still provided to developing countries, and focusing it exclusively on elimination of fossil energy use. Countries unwilling to accept such assistance, could perhaps be referred to the WTO, since they could clearly be seen to be lowering their production costs by using cheap fossil fuel and thus imposing the costs of global warming on the rest of us.

It might also be helpful to have a "truth and reconciliation" Conference at some stage, that would document the culpability of the developed countries for current levels of ACO2 (see Table 1). There does not seem to be any realistic possibility of getting developed countries to pay for, or sequester permanently, the massive amounts of carbon that they have added to the atmosphere, but they could at least acknowledge the damage they have done: Thus changing the atmosphere for international assistance to reduce AFCO2TA from generosity to reparations.

Chapter 12: Action Program

The key motivation for writing this book was the feeling that while there is a vast, informative and well documented literature on the nature and scope of the global warming problem, this same literature is relatively sparse in terms of policy recommendations.

An action program can be thought of in three parts:

i)   "Personal Virtue" as discussed in Chapter 3.

ii) Understanding the problem and appropriate policy responses, and

iii) Political agitation.

<u>Understanding the Problem</u>: If this is the first book you have read on global warming or you are not adequately convinced of the problem, reading the remaining chapters might help but all of the following books state the problem excellently: *The Weather Makers*, by Tim Flannery, *Field Notes From A Catastrophe*, by Elizabeth Kolbert, *An Inconvenient Truth*, by Al Gore, *Heat: How to Stop the Planet from Burning*, by George Monbiot, *Boiling Point* by Ross Gelbspan, *Hell and High Water* by Joseph Romm, *The Rough Guide to Climate Change* by Robert Henson, and *The Carbon War* by Jeremy Leggett.

<u>Appropriate Policy Responses</u>: Ross Gelbspan maintains a website dedicated to global warming at www.heatisonline.org/main.cfm including a link to "Global Solution". A three pronged policy action is proposed:

- **In industrial countries, the withdrawal of subsidies from fossil fuels and the establishment of equivalent subsidies for clean energy sources;**

- **The creation of a large fund -- perhaps through a small tax on global commerce -- to transfer clean energy technologies to developing countries; and,**

- **The incorporation within the Kyoto framework of a progressively more stringent Fossil Fuel Efficiency Standard that rises by 5 percent per year**.

A web-site that focuses on the carbon tax proposal is at www. carbontax.org. This web site advocates two variations of the revenue neutral carbon tax proposal:

"Two primary return approaches are being discussed. One would rebate the revenues directly through regular (e.g., monthly) equal dividends to all U.S. residents. In effect, every resident would receive equal, identical slices of the total revenue pie. Just such a program has operated in Alaska for three decades, providing residents with annual dividends from the state's North Slope oil revenues.

In the other method, each dollar of carbon tax revenue would trigger a dollar's worth of reduction in existing taxes such as the federal payroll tax or state sales taxes. As carbon-tax revenues are phased in (with the tax rates rising gradually but steadily, to allow a smooth transition), existing taxes will be phased out and, in some cases, eliminated. This "tax-shift" approach, while less direct than the dividend method, would also ensure that the carbon tax is revenue-neutral."

This book has argued for the first option.

See also Chapter 14 "Hansen on Climate".

It is very important that those of us concerned to address the problem of global warming not get involved in childish squabbles about "who had the best idea", or "who said what first". The remnants of the Global Climate Coalition and the Enterprise Institute and other flacks would like nothing better than to initiate a debate as to which policy to adopt, while doing nothing pending outcome of the debate. *Timing is now of the essence*, we should settle for the constructive policy that can be implemented first; and refine the policy later as we see the need for improvements.

So in a spirit of learning from each other, let me say that the above are all good suggestions. In particular the second and third bullets provide ideas for international cooperation, and could well serve as simple additions to the policy portfolio suggested below. In essence I have given up on international agreements, so all suggestions in this area are welcome.

With regard to the first bullet, the removal of subsidies from fossil fuels is a "no-brainer" (no offense intended), this has to cover both direct subsidies, and "administrative subsidies" such as below market lease rates, and even failure to collect royalty payments. *It makes no sense to subsidies global warming,* as we are doing, and have been doing. Truly a "no-brainer", and a suggestion explicitly included in the recommended policy portfolio below.

Subsidies may be a little more subtle. Clearly some encouragement for clean energy source (aka fossil-free energy) is needed. I have three concerns about subsidies:

i)   It is difficult to give equivalent subsidies to different technologies (unless the subsidy is, say per unit of electricity generated, in which case the subsidy is very like a "negative tax", fine but it is simpler to raise the positive carbon tax),

ii) If distinct subsidies are given for different technologies, then each technology has an incentive to lobby, and to buy the votes of key politicians, thus corrupting the democratic process, and

iii) A subsidy once given may be hard to withdraw, especially if a symbiotic relationship is established between industries and key legislators.

Yes, certainly we need to give support to clean energy however there may be room for useful debate as to how to give it: As a matter of practical politics, and given the urgency of doing something, if we can get a subsidy through before a tax increase, let's go with the subsidy!

Going beyond the above three bullet plan, what then can we suggest in terms of an action plan for let us say, the United States?

Firstly, and most clearly, we have to get rid of the Bush administration: It is political and rotten to the core. Far from America being able to exercise international leadership and "soft power", this administration has turned the phrases American "leadership" and "soft power" into oxymorons. The administration simply has no credibility: Either that it wishes to do the right thing, or could do the right thing if it tried.

To mobilize market forces (on which any successful program has to depend) we need to *minimize uncertainty* for investors and market participants[111]. This makes it essential that any program to control global warming be crystal clear as to the objectives, and how it is expected that they will be attained.

Thus *it is urgent that the State of the Union in 2009 commit America to eliminating AFCO2TA as quickly as possible*, because we know ACO2 concentration cause global warming: The rate of reduction to be slowed down only so as to avoid the most severe economic dislocations.

En route to a fossil-free economy, develop and demonstrate the capture and sequestration of carbon as a new technology. Having achieved a zero AFCO2TA economy, we will re-evaluate the capture and sequester strategy in the light of experience. Either accepting this as equivalent to not using fossil fuels, or discounting capture and sequester to the point that we reach a truly fossil-free economy.

If a date is mentioned, say 2030, it should be clear that if the opportunity arises we will be stop AFCO2TA before that date.

Contrast the above statement with the President's anodyne 2007 State of the Union:

"America is on the verge of technological breakthroughs that will enable us to live our lives less dependent on oil. And these technologies will help us be better stewards of the environment, and they will help us to confront the serious challenge of global climate change."

There is nothing in this latter statement that provides guidance to investors or indeed consumers despite acknowledging "the serious challenge of global climate change" it says that technological breakthroughs will soon solve the problem. ….. The problem is not recognized, and accordingly no relevant policies are proposed[112].

Reverting to the needed policy changes: The public commitment to eliminating AFCO2TA is crucial, without it, the proposed actions could appear random and ad hoc. Also this statement makes it clear that the commitment is not dependent on the actions of other nations. The American leadership considers the problem so severe that it will take action even if other nations do not: A national application of what Vice-President Chaney calls "personal virtue". Leading by example, is the best way for America to regain a respected voice in international discussions.

The public commitment to eliminating AFCO2TA should be accompanied by official "science based" year by year projections of:

i) expected levels of AFCO2TA by the U.S. and other leading polluters,

ii) absolute levels of ACO2 in ppm,

iii) estimated global temperature, and

iv) expected major impacts.

These estimates would serve two important purposes. They would warn how far the U.S. acting alone fails to stem global warming, thus putting pressure on others to adopt similar policies, and they will allow us to see the magnitude of errors in the scientific projections, that underlie our basic sense of urgency, or lack thereof. (See Chapter 15, Keeping Tabs).

Perhaps having to wait at the national level until January 2009 is a blessing in disguise. We can use the next year to reach consensus on what should be done.

At the level of the individual state, we can in any case immediately promote the "Californian Plan" of encouraging utilities to work with consumers to increase the efficiency of electricity utilization (as discussed in Chapter 3, Personal Virtue). In California, a 50% increase in electricity rates, coupled with utilities help and advice on conserving electricity resulted in about a 40% drop in electricity usage per person compared to the nation as a whole, and this has been done, entirely on the basis of using existing technologies.

The House and Senate should establish a *joint bipartisan* Caucus on Global Warming. The primary objective of which would be to educate caucus members on the evidence for global warming, likely impacts and policy options. It is essential that our legislators become much better informed on global warming, and that a partisan split be avoided if at all possible. Education should take the form both of speakers and field visits to see the impact of global warming at first hand[113].

Nancy Pelosi, Leader of the House, has set up a Select Committee on Energy Independence and Global Warming, this is a very useful initiative within the committee structure of the House. In particular it should ensure that all relevant legislative proposals are examined from the perspective of "what do they mean for energy independence and global warming?" It is particularly useful that energy independence is coupled to global warming this should prevent energy independence being pursued at the expense of global warming, and ensure that liquid-coal proposals die in committee. However, there are also some dangers:

i) Politically this may be seen as a Democratic attempt to "capture" the global warming issue. Global warming is much too dangerous to be treated as a partisan issue.

ii) It may lead to non-committee members losing interest in global warming since "we have another committee dealing with that".

iii) In part, this new committee seems to have been established due to Nancy Pelosi's impatience with the apparent passivity of the existing Energy and Commerce Committee. In any case, stung by the obvious overlap, John Dingell, Chairman of the House Energy and Commerce Committee has introduced legislation to tax carbon ($10 a ton in the first year rising to $50 a ton in the fifth year, and using some of the tax to increase the earned income-tax credit, and other good works, see Chapter 14).

It is important that in addition to the Select Committee there be an avenue for all legislators to be educated on the global warming crisis.

In the next 12 months, Congress should unfund the Iraq war that is a dangerous distraction, strike hydrogen research from the budget, and remove the tariff on ethanol. It should hold additional hearings on global warming, focused on the efforts by the administration to prevent scientists speaking, whether there was a concerted effort by the media to confuse the public, and the role of the Global Climate Coalition and industry supported think-tanks in obscuring the extent of the global warming we are experiencing. In addition Congress could add a number of key actions by the nefarious practice of ear marks.

Key ear-markable *studies* might include:

i) A reworking of the IPCC panel projections to calibrate them not only by chronological time, but current and cumulative fossil CO_2 emissions, global temperature, sea level, ocean sequestration of CO_2 and associated pH, and status of the Greenland and Antarctic ice sheets.

ii) A careful examination of the IPCC scenarios, that underlie IPCC projections, and examination of plausibility of the economic behavior and political decisions in the scenarios.

iii) The earliest that the U.S. could eliminate AFCO2TA.

iv) Regulatory barriers to wind, nuclear and solar-thermal power generation.

Key *research* to be ear-marked might include funding:

i) plug-in hybrids,

ii) ligno-cellulosic ethanol and diesel,

iii) HVDC transmission systems,

iv) real time pricing of electricity,

v) economic models to support adaptation and mitigation policies,

vi) feasibility studies for flying wind-farms,

vii) research to determine the feasibility and cost of alternative geo-engineering proposals, and

viii) research, development and demonstration of carbon capture and sequestration, both from flue gasses (with or without algae) and directly from the atmosphere.

Discussions could usefully be initiated with the IEA and OECD as to the possibility that they would provide secretariat services to support international collaboration to eliminate AFCO2TA. If the IEA proved negative to this idea, thought could be given as to whether there are alternative forms for an international organization that would attract widespread respect and have the authority to impose a world-wide ban of industrial practices linked to global warming.

The World Bank and IMF could be asked to comment on the plausibility of the assumptions used in creating the IPCC scenarios.

Finally, these remaining 12-months of the Bush presidency would allow full discussion of the following policy proposals to be implemented in early 2009. This discussion should include opinions from the IPCC modelers as to the impact, if any, of the individual elements of the proposed action program.

Additional Policy Proposals:

Explain the Program: It is very important that the electorate understand the need for the program, and how the various components fit together. It is to be expected that USCAP and others likely to be affected by the new policies will try to undermine them and confuse the public. This is easily done, and needs to be met with and at least equal effort by proponents of the program. The President and members of the Global Warming Caucus should use all "bully-pulpits" as become available.

Domestic Energy: Ban manufacture of incandescent bulbs, and low efficiency household appliances. This will require support for recycling of florescent bulbs, to avoid the mercury they contain leaking into the environment.

Electricity Generation: Ban construction of new fossil-fired generating plants. Yes there may be electrical blackouts, but it is likely that the doubling in price of electricity will lead to very slow growth, if any, in demand for a several years, and real-time pricing of electricity as introduced will lead to low priority uses of electricity being switched off, rather than the whole system going down.

Personal Virtue: Continue with Californian-style support for increased efficiency in the use of electricity, at the state level.

Construction: Require all new and rebuilt residential, office and retail construction to meet *passivhause* specifications. Minimize the use of cement.

Fossil Free Electricity: Remove regulatory barriers to creation of wind-farms, nuclear and solar-thermal power plants.

Trains: Introduce high speed passenger trains, and electrify all rail tracks. Ban use of diesel locomotives on electrified track.

Automobile Standards: Require 10% of cars sold in 2014 to be plug-in hybrids, rising to 100% in 2024. (This is a sop to Detroit to try to catch-up, after being distracted by the Bush hydrogen mirage).

Carbon Credits: Ban trade in privately created carbon credits. (As argued in Chapter 4, privately created carbon credits are a distraction that never results in the removal of carbon from the carbon cycle).

Taxation: *Impose a $250 ton of carbon tax on fossil fuels* (oil and natural gas used in the chemical industry for non-biodegradable products, to be exempted), while dropping all energy subsidies and reducing the payroll tax, as suggested in Chapter 7. Note that *this is the key provision that will provide a level playing field enabling different technologies to be fairly evaluated.* We do not propose individual subsidies for fossil-free technologies, since a tax $250 a ton of carbon *is equivalent to a massive subsidy to all fossil-free technologies.*

Subsidy: *Purchase up to 1,000 tons of carbon sequestered annually, at a maximum price of $400 per ton. Purchase to be by Dutch auction.* This subsidy would require EPA regulations and inspection. It would be repayable in the event of loss of sequestered CO_2. Carbon sequestration is a proven technology (see Box 2) however it is not clear that it can be done economically. If the cost of sequestration can be brought down to $200, or better $ 100, per ton of carbon, then sequestration (i.e. withdrawal) of carbon from the carbon cycle might be economic, as for instance burning bio-carbon to produce electricity, and collecting the flue gases for sequestration. This purchase offer is to encourage innovation.

Subsidies: Remove blending subsidies and tariff on bio- ethanol. It is likely that the new tax on fossil-carbon will make ethanol attractive however there is no need to produce it domestically if it can be imported more cheaply.

It is likely that these twin actions will result in substantial ethanol imports.

Subsidies: Remove subsidies on photo-voltaic cells.

If doubling the price of electricity is not enough to make photo-voltaic cells economic, we should wait until research and development reduces the cost to the point that they become economic.

Subsidies: Congressman John Dingell's draft carbon tax legislation provides for a reduction in the proportion of mortgage interest payments that will be tax deductible for larger homes. This is obviously a move in the right direction, although it would be improved by being tied to the energy efficiency of the home design.

Transmission: Begin planning/feasibility studies of needed HVDC grid, and who will provide, fund and manage this service.

Research: Support particularly the development of real-time electricity pricing, with capacity for household devices to be switched on or off in response to electricity prices; and geo-engineering proposals.

Electrical Storage: Begin identification of pumped storage locations.

Class-Action Suits: The way should be cleared for class action suits based on actions of the Global Climate Coalition, USCAP, Enterprise Institute and other front organizations to be pursued against the deep-pockets that funded their activities.

Foreign Assistance: Consolidate all foreign aid (including military assistance) into one fund to be used to help developing countries to shift from fossil based power production to cleaner technologies, including nuclear.

International Leadership: Announce commitment to elimination of AFCO2TA by the U.S. before 2030, with accompanying year by year emission targets. Host an international conference to discuss feasibility of this goal, willingness of others to adopt the goal, and ideas for disciplining countries that ignore the contribution that they are making to global warming.

Note that our approach to policy should be heuristic, learning by doing. We should not hesitate to change these policies in the light of experience. Some may need to be cancelled, others expanded, tax and subsidy rates should be reviewed, as well as funding levels for infrastructural investments, levels of research support, and so on. The most important thing is to take the full portfolio of actions **NOW**.

Political Agitation: Clearly the above policy proposals need national legislative action, which in turn means that politicians need to be convinced that the electorate wants these changes made.

As an *individual* you can watch the news, newspapers and magazines for articles that refer to global warming or proposed policy actions. You can then write to local and national papers (different wording in each letter). These may well not be published, but they indicate to the media your interest in the subject. You can also send copies of the best of your letters to your Representative and Senators. www.fcnl.org click on "Contact Congress" makes it easy to write to your representatives. It is a simple matter to copy a letter into the space provided, perhaps with the introduction "You may be interested to know that I have just written the following letter to ....," and perhaps ending with "I urge you to read Chapter 12 of "Global Warming: The Answer" (!). It is the whole package that we need to push.

The web-site www.carbontax.org monitors developments with respect to a revenue neutral, carbon tax. The site favors achieving revenue neutrality by lowering other tax rates, but it clearly understands the need to raise the price of carbon, without the windfall gains to energy companies that are implied by C&T.

I have no experience with the blogosphere but the Gelbspan web-site mentioned above has a good coverage of breaking environmental news, and links to the environmental web-community. These sites are both interesting and encouraging, however this leaves you interacting with the convinced, when we need to be interacting with the unconvinced or those who believe that they can be indifferent.

You can look for opportunities where political candidates are campaigning, attend events, and ask firstly "do you believe that global warming is occurring?" and then "how do you feel about a revenue neutral carbon tax?" or "which books on global warming have you read?" Be specific, don't give them an opportunity to recite some stump-speech.

If you make donations to environmental organizations (or political parties) check their position on the revenue neutral carbon tax, and nuclear power. … We have to encourage nuclear power until we have dispensed with fossil fuels that are a much graver threat.

If you make any charity donations, think about re-directing them to global warming activist groups.

Beyond these activities that you can undertake as an individual, you can think of *increasing global warming awareness* within your social or religious community. You can lend people books, see if others are interested in organizing a discussion group, and then widen this to lobby as a group. If you look round you will probably find local environmental activist groups concerned with local issues (wetlands, forest preservation, urban sprawl, etc.) You can join such groups, or get speakers for your discussion group, and then push them as to why they do not put equal emphasis on global warming, which will make all other problems moot in the near future.

There is every reason to believe that the train has left the station. If the relaxed Stern/IPCC view that the train is in the station and will be for several years turns out to be right, prompt and comprehensive action now may avert disaster. If we have passed a key (or several key) tipping point(s), prompt action is needed to minimize the disaster.

Chapter 13: Hansen on Climate

On April 26th, 2007 Dr. James Hansen made a presentation to the Select Committee on Energy Independence and Global Warming of the House of Representatives. It is a pity that he was not granted a much larger audience. *No legislator should be unaware of what he said.* Despite being one of (probably the) leading climate scientist in government employ, he had to give his testimony as a private citizen, since he felt it incumbent upon himself to speak about policy, and the urgency of the problem of global warming. By implication his views did not coincide with those of his politically appointed supervisors, or he would have been able to speak on behalf of NASA (National Aeronautical and Space Agency).

Readers are urged to read his testimony *Dangerous Human-Made Interference with Climate* that can be downloaded from http://www. columbia.edu/~jeh1/testimony_26april2007.pdf. Readers should have no difficulty in following Dr. Hansen's presentation. It may be interesting to compare and contrast some of his main points with ideas in this book.

Tipping Points: By tipping points Dr. Hansen means positive feed-back loops, where a rise in temperature triggers a response that leads to further temperature rises. We have mentioned melting glaciers, melting of the permafrost, and forest fires. Dr Hansen focuses on melting ice:

"For humanity itself, the greatest threat is the likely demise of the West Antarctic ice sheet as it is attacked from below by a warming ocean and above by increased surface melt. There is increasing realization that sea level rise this century may be measured in meters if we follow business-as-usual fossil fuel emissions." (p.3)

Coupled with this, he suggests that climate models have probably miss-represented historical evidence, in that historically forcing[114] has been quite modest over millennia. Glacial melting has similarly been slow (not to say glacial), and models have tended to reflect this despite the fact that our "forcing" is far faster than has previously been experience. Hansen suggests that models of glacial melt should be driven not by the passage of time, but the level of "forcing", suggesting that current models have probably significantly over-estimated the time frame for (underestimated the rapidity of) glacial melting and sea level rise. The consensus model generates sea level rise is about a foot over the next century.

Specifically Dr. Hansen says, "At the end of the last ice age sea level rose more than 100 m in less than 10,000 years, thus more than 1 m per century on average. At times during this deglaciation, sea level rose as fast as 4-5 m per century" (p.11): That is as much as *1.5 feet per decade*. And this was with much lower levels of forcing than are now being provided, however it was probably associated with release of water down the St Laurence when an ice wall holding melt water under the Laurentide ice sheet broke. Fortunately we do not have any known large glacial lakes above sea level waiting to be released.

This concern is echoed in *Hell and High Water* by Joseph Romm, "'The recent sea-ice retreat is larger than any of the (19) IPCC [climate] models', Tore Furevik pointed out in a November 2005 talk on climate-system feedbacks. He is deputy director of Norway's Bjerkness Center for Climatic Research. Once again, the models on which the IPCC bases its conclusions appears to be 'too conservative'" (p.78).

The problem of deglacination is not only the impact on the sea level (although that is bad enough) but also it creates a feed-back loop (or "tipping point") as rock or ocean that used to be covered in ice and reflected a high proportion of incoming energy back into space, is exposed, and thus absorbs much more of the incoming energy.

The adjustments that IPCC models predict will need to be made over the next century *may need to be made over the next decade or two*.

This change in the time scale, affects the urgency of policy change, but not the substance. We have already called for an *immediate* carbon tax of $250 per ton, and supporting measures to minimized AFCO2TA. Perhaps we should modify the recommendation to a tax of *at least* $250 per ton.

The Tipping Point of primary concern to Dr. Hansen is a temperature 1°C, above year 2000 temperatures (already 7 years ago) or 450 ppm of ACO2:

"….the upshot of crystallizing science is that the 'safe' global temperature level is, at most, about 1°C greater than year 2000 temperature. It may be less, indeed, I suspect that it is less, but that does not alter our conclusions."

"A 1°C limit on added global warming implies a CO_2 ceiling of about 450 ppm (reference A). There is some 'play' in the CO_2 ceiling due to other human-made climate forcings that cause warming, especially methane, nitrous oxide, and 'black soot'. The 'alternative scenario' (Hansen et al., Proc. Natl. Acad. Sci., 97, 9875-9880, 2000), designed to keep additional warming under 1°C, has CO_2 peaking at 475 ppm via an assumed large reduction of CH_4 (methane). However, human-made sulfate aerosols, which have a cooling effect, are likely to decrease and tend to offset reductions of positive non-CO_2 forcings. Therefore 450 ppm is a good first estimate of the maximum allowable CO_2. *Indeed, if recent mass loss in Antarctica is the beginning of a growing trend, it is likely that even 450 ppm is excessive and dangerous.*" (p. 17) (emphasis added).

If glacial melting is driven by temperature, rather than ppm, then the figure to keep our eye on is the 1°C rise above the temperature in 2000. Dr. Hansen warns us about:

"Climate response time. A practical difficulty with climate change arises from the fact that the climate system does not respond immediately to climate forcings. Figure 1 shows the climate response to a forcing introduced at time t = 0. It requires about 30 years for 50% of the eventual (equilibrium) global warming to be achieved, about 250 years for 75% of the response, and perhaps a millennium for 90% of the surface response." (p. 7)

It thus appears that if we had stopped AFCO2TA in 2000, it would be 2050 before half or the eventual (equilibrium) global warming was evident. We don't know how much further temperature would rise in those 50 years, but there are disquieting results that hint this could be over 1°C. The IPCC models give a "sensitivity" within 1°C to 3°C[115].

"Sensitivity" is the increase in temperature at equilibrium from pre-industrial times, given a doubling of ACO2 to 560 ppm[116]. With linear interpolation we can calculate Table 7.

Table 7: Linear Interpolation of Sensitivity

Year	ACO2	Sensitivity	Change from 1.6°C
1850	280	0.0	-1.6
2000	370	0.96	-0.64
2007	384	1.11	-0.49
?	450	1.82	0.22
?	560	3.0	1.4

Since the actual temperature rise from pre-industrial to 2000 has been about 0.6°C, this suggests (however roughly) that without any further AFCO2TA after 2000, temperature would have continued to rise another 0.3 to 0.4°C.

It is worth taking time to understand exactly what Table 7 is saying. The first two columns are self-evident. Year is the relevant year, and ACO2 is the reported concentration of atmospheric CO2 in ppm, the two question marks indicating that we do not know in which year the corresponding levels of ACO2 will be achieved. The sensitivity column is simply a linear interpolation knowing that in 1850 (ACO2 = 280 ppm) sensitivity was zero, and at 560 ppm it is expected to be 3.0 (IPPC central estimate). Thus the rate of change in sensitivity per unit change in ACO2 is estimated to be:

$$\text{Change in sensitivity/change in ACO2} = 3/280$$
$$= 0.01071$$

(280 is not the ACO2 in 1850, but the difference between 560 and 280).

For 2000 this yields an interpolated sensitivity of:

Sensitivity = rate of change*change in ACO2(ppm)
= 0.0107*90
= 0.963

(Where the 90 is the change in ACO2 from 1850 to 2000).

The final column accepts Dr. Hansen's estimate that a further 1°C beyond the temperature in 2006, may be taken as likely to lead to a tipping point. Since the temperature in 2000 has been reported as 0.6°C above the pre-industrial level, *Dr. Hansen's estimate is 1.6°C above the pre-industrial level.* Now relating this to estimated sensitivity at various concentrations of ACO2, we get the numbers in the last column. In particular for 2007, with an interpolated sensitivity of 1.11 only a rise of 0.49°C remains before hitting Dr. Hansen's suggested limit of 1.6°C above pre-industrial levels. In short this argument suggests that we may have only about half as much time to abandon AFCO2TA as suggested by Dr. Hansen[117].

This difference in estimation of severity of the problem leaves basic agreement on the policy recommendations: *We need to take action immediately, if not sooner.*

Policy Recommendations: Dr. Hansen's policy recommendations have substantial overlap with those presented in this book, and also interesting differences. The following is a long quote that has all been put in italics to emphasize the continuity of the quote:

"An outline of the strategy that humanity must follow to avoid dangerous climate change emerges from the above boundary conditions. It is a four-point strategy (following tables).

Outline of Solution

1. Coal only in Power Plants with Sequestration
(Phase out old technology. Timetable TBD)

2   *Stretch Conventional Gas and Oil*
    (Via Incentives(Carbon Tax)& Standards)
    (Avoid unconventional Fossil Fuels)

3. *Reduce non-CO2 Climate Forcings*
    (Methane, Black Soot, Nitrous Oxide)

4. *Draw Down Atmospheric CO2*
    (Improve Agricultural & Forest Practices)
    (Perhaps Biofuel-Powered Plants)

Methods to Reduce CO2 Emissions

1. *Energy Efficiency & Conservation*
    (More Efficient Technology)
    (Life Style Changes)

2. *Renewable & CO2-Free Energy*
    (Hydro)
    (Solar, Wind Geothermal)
    (Nuclear)

3. *CO2 Capture and Sequestration*
    -> <u>No Silver Bullet</u>
    -> <u>All Three are Essential</u>

A. Coal and Unconventional Fossil Fuels

First, coal and unconventional fossil fuels must be used only with carbon capture and sequestration. Existing coal-fired power plants must be phased out over the next few decades. This is the primary requirement for avoiding 'a different planet'.

It is probably impractical to prevent use of most of the easily extractable oil and its use in small mobile sources. This makes it essential to use the huge coal resource in a way such that the CO2 can be captured, and, indeed, the logical use of coal is in power plants. It is important to recognize that a substantial fraction of the CO2 emitted, if it is not captured, will remain in the air for an eternity.

Thus the most critical action for saving the planet at this time, I believe, is to prevent construction of additional coal-fired power plants without CO2 capture capability. As governments around the world, not only in the United States, China and India, fail to appreciate this situation, it is important that citizens draw attention to the issue.

B. Stretching Oil and Gas with a Carbon Tax

Oil and gas must be 'stretched' so as to cover needs for mobile fuels during the transition period to the next phase of the industrial era 'beyond petroleum'. This 'stretching', almost surely, can only be achieved if there is a continually rising price on carbon emissions. Innovations will be unleashed if industry realizes that this rising price is certain. Efficiency standards, for vehicles, buildings, appliances, and lighting are needed, as well as a carbon price. The carbon tax will also avert the threat of emissions from unconventional fossil fuels, such as tar shale.

C. Drawing Down Atmospheric CO2

Because CO2 is already near the dangerous level, steps must be taken to 'draw down' atmospheric CO2. Farming and forestry practices that enhance carbon retention and storage in the soil and biosphere should be supported.

In addition, burning biofuels in power plants with carbon capture and sequestration could draw down atmospheric CO2[118] in effect putting anthropogenic CO2 back underground where it came from. CO2 sequestered beneath ocean sediments is inherently stable[119], and other safe geologic sites may also be available.

This use of biofuels in a power plant, which would draw down atmospheric CO2, should be contrasted with use of corn-based ethanol to power vehicles. The latter process still results in large increases of atmospheric CO2, increases food prices worldwide, and results in deforestation and poor agricultural practices as greater land area is pressed into service. In the use of biofuels for power plants, mentioned above, we would envisage use of cellulosic fibers and native grasses harvested with non-till practices. Limited land availability may make it difficult for biofuels to be the long-term solution for vehicle propulsion.

D. Non-CO2 Climate Forcings

A reduction of non-CO2 forcings can be a significant help in achieving the climate forcings needed to keep climate change within given bounds. Reduction of non-CO2 forcings has benefits for human health and agriculture[120], as well as for climate. Reduction of non-CO2 forcings is especially effective in limiting Arctic climate change (reference A)." (p. 17)

<u>Comment</u>: For convenient reference Dr. Hansen's outline solution is repeated:

Outline of Solution

1. *Coal only in Power Plants with Sequestration*
    (Phase out old technology. Timetable TBD)

2. *Stretch Conventional Gas and Oil*
    (Via Incentives(Carbon tax)& Standards)
    (Avoid unconventional Fossil Fuels)

3. *Reduce non-CO2 Climate Forcings*
    (Methane, Black Soot, Nitrous Oxide)

4. *Draw Down Atmospheric CO2*
    (Improve Agricultural & Forest Practices)
    (Perhaps Biofuel-Powered Plants)

These are commendably straight forward and actionable recommendations. Differences in emphasis are:

i) Dr. Hansen only recommends using a carbon tax on conventional oil and gas, relying on regulation to phase out coal power plants without sequestration. Clearly we are headed in the same direction. I would stand by the overall carbon tax, as providing an even playing field, and inhibiting the use of unconventional fossil fuels, such as shale and oil-sands. It is possible that we should take a leaf out of Dr. Hansen's book, and have a separate tax for petroleum and natural gas, since even a $250 ton of carbon tax, does not give a very significant incentive to economize on the more energy intensive fuels. Probably the carbon tax would be sufficient to ensure that no more coal power plants without capture would be proposed. However, *his suggestion of a simple ban on such new plants would be a useful reinforcement for the policy.*

ii) Dr. Hansen is cryptic on sequestration. It is not clear whether he thinks coal power plants with sequestration would be economic, or whether this is a polite way of saying "no more coal plants" until sequestration costs are brought down. Recommendations in the last chapter provided for incentives to encourage the development of cheaper sequestration technologies.

iii) Dr. Hansen's TBD (to be decided) timetable should surely be replace by ASP (as soon as possible)!

iv) Dr. Hansen makes no mention as to what is to be done with the revenue from the carbon tax. As argued earlier (Chapter 7) it is desirable to give this back to the citizenry via a rebate to registered voters so as to ease the political acceptability of a new tax.

v) Adequate carbon (and if necessary gasoline) taxes should heighten the demand for low mpg vehicle, however Dr. Hansen is right that there are many for whom price is

141

irrelevant, so mpg standards to reinforce tax policy are likely to be needed. Such standards will almost certainly meet protests from the American auto-companies that proposed standards are impossible to meet[121]. If we have to choose between the car companies and the environment, the choice is simple. We need our car companies to stop lobbying, and start engineering. If they cannot make more efficient cars they will be driven out of business by competitors that can. A useful application of Dr. Hansen's suggestion for standards, would be to progressively raise the mpg standard for licensing cars, thus gradually forcing the least efficient cars off the road.

vi) The proposal to "avoid unconventional fossil fuels" probably refers primarily to the proposal, under the rubric of "energy independence", for liquid-coal: Production of liquid fuel from coal. This has already been discussed in Chapter 5 (see especially Table 5). We can whole heartedly endorse Dr. Hansen's recommendation. Liquid-coal is a luddite proposal, well able to undo all other potential gains. (Again the carbon tax would go a long way to making liquid-coal unattractive).

vii) We have made no policy proposal to reduce non-CO_2 forcing, beyond noting that these additional pollutants could be subject to pollutant specific taxes, in parallel with the carbon tax. It would be useful for Dr. Hansen to spell out the technologies, or other policy changes that could be used to reduce this additional pollution.

viii) We have not discussed improved forestry and agricultural practices, but to the extent that they can increase the sequestered CO_2, they are to be welcomed.

Methods to Reduce CO2 Emissions

1. *Energy Efficiency & Conservation*
   (More Efficient Technology)
   (Life Style Changes)

2. *Renewable & CO2-Free Energy*
   (Hydro)
   (Solar, Wind Geothermal)
   (Nuclear)

3. *CO2 Capture and Sequestration*
   -> *No Silver Bullet*
   -> *All Three are Essential*

ix) We have discussed technology in Chapter 9 and personal virtue in Chapter 3.

x) There are many sources of renewable energy. A $250 carbon tax would enable the fossil-free technologies to flourish.

xi) We endorse Dr. Hansen's recommendation "All Three are Essential" and NOW. Indeed we would shorten this to "**all are essential,** *NOW*".

Summary: Six things stand out from this testimony:

i) The eminence of the person testifying,

ii) That the testimony was given as an individual,

iii) The sense of urgency,

iv) The concreteness of the proposed actions,

v) The modest size of the listening audience, and

vi) The almost total failure of Congress to react to what it had heard[122].

Given the testimony, the absence of any response by the relevant lead government agency is appalling. If Dr. Hansen has it wrong, we would expect that NASA would provide rebutting testimony. If he is right, we would expect that NASA would approve of his speaking on behalf of the agency, at least on the scientific evidence on the nature of the problem. Instead there was a deafening silence.

What can be more concrete than the recommendation that we build no new coal plants without sequestration? If Congress had seen fit to ban any new coal-fired generating plants without sequestration, it would have brought the whole question of global warming and what we are going to do about it, center stage.

Not only has Congress not adopted the policies advocated by Dr. Hansen, but under the guise of "energy independence" it seems set to provide $10 billion to support liquid-coal (without sequestration) which would *double* the rate of AFCO2TA per mile driven with the new fuel! And against which Dr. Hansen explicitly warned.

As discussed in the next chapter, this Congress seems to be the government we deserve.

Chapter 14: Spaceship Titanic

"The lesson is to avoid doing too much, too fast",
Stern Review.

This has been a hard chapter to write, since each day the papers seem to report yet another idiot striving to be recognized (See Box 13); or an established idiot trying to reassert his (they are almost all male) supremacy.

We are all passengers on spaceship Titanic, and nothing that the captain, crew or passengers are doing is reassuring:

- The White House is struggling to complete 16 lost years[123] with no, to put it mildly, great sense of urgency. As President Bush said in the 2007 State of the Union (Feb. 2007)[124] "Addressing global climate change will require a sustained effort, over many generations. My approach recognizes that sustained economic growth is the solution, not the problem" ….."America is on the verge of technological breakthroughs that will enable us to live our lives less dependent on oil. And these technologies will help us be better stewards of the environment, and they will help us to confront the serious challenge of global climate change." This is a *generational problem*, the heart of which is to make us less dependent on oil. Give me a break! The "new technologies" basically involve using coal as an oil substitute (a 1920's technology), that *doubles the emissions* compared to using gasoline!

- The White House has switched the target from rate of fossil CO2 emissions to "energy efficiency", or "rate of increase in fossil CO2 emissions per unit of GDP". All this requires is that GDP grow faster than fossil carbon emissions. This is not even stabilizing fossil CO2 emissions, let alone eliminating them. One can only conclude that there is a basic lack of understanding by the White House of the challenge we face. I have a new bumper sticker *"Warning: It is dangerous to share a planet with the current White House."*

- Despite the President's announcement that "NASA will invest over $120 million in the next three years in research on the natural carbon cycle, climate modeling, and the link between atmospheric chemistry and climate" (7/13/2001) NASA administrator Michael Griffin (on PBS, 5/31/2007): "I have no doubt that global - that a trend of global warming exists. I am not sure that it is fair to say that it is a problem we must wrestle with. To assume that it is a problem is to assume that the state of the Earth's climate today is the optimal climate, the best climate that we could have or ever have had, and that we need to take steps to make sure that it doesn't change. I don't think it's within the power of human beings to assure that the climate does not change, as millions of years of history have shown. And second of all, I guess I would ask which human beings - where and when - are to be accorded the privilege of deciding that this particular climate that we have right here today, right now, is the best climate for all other human beings. I think that's a rather arrogant position for people to take." *That is the NASA administrator!* The argument of climate experts is not that we can control climate, or that the present climate is optimal, but that we can (and are) making it warmer and climate will undoubtedly get worse if we do not stop AFCO2TA. Is he really indifferent as to whether there is a 20 foot sea level rise? NASA has a $16.5 billion a year research program, and a commitment by the President to spend $40 million a year on climate issues, yet the administrator does not think global warming is a problem? It is not a question of being "within the power of human being to assure that the climate does not change": It is that anyone who turns on a (fossil) light switch affects the climate. We all have the power to change the climate that is the problem. "Heck of a job, Griffin!".

- Note the President's $120 million over three years, amounts to about 0.24% of the NASA research budget. Reinforcing the concern that the lack of seriousness traces all the way to the White House.

- In May the Associated Press reported that the Bush administration was scaling back expenditures on measuring global warming from space. Originally it was agreed that to economize one satellite system could be used to meet the needs of the Pentagon, NOAA (National Oceanographic and Atmospheric Agency) and NASA. The management of the system was entrusted to the Pentagon, that allowed a 100% cost overrun by the defense contractor, then to economize again the Pentagon (and White House) decided to remove the very features that would have made the system useful to NOAA and NASA!

- Tony Blair and the whole British Cabinet are using carbon credits in the belief that this can offset fossil carbon released in official travel (130+ tons for Tony Blair in 2005)[125]. *They just don't get it!* (see Chapter 4).

- Britain has established the objective of reducing CO2 emissions by 60% by 2050, yet is building seven new runways at commercial air-ports. Again reductions in CO2 emissions, not fossil CO2 emissions … *they just don't get it!*

- Al Gore is chairman of Generation Investment Management a company that sells carbon credits[126] (including to himself), amongst other things. *Does he begin to understand what his company is doing?* It is giving people (including himself) the impression that they are offsetting AFCO2TA, when they are not.

- China is going full speed ahead in the construction of coal fired generating plants (Box 9), under a global warming policy that mirrors Bush's belief that economic growth is the answer, not the problem.

So much for the captain(s), now about the crew of scientists, other experts, politicians and the media:

- The media are absolutely crucial since they report, and can easily distort the scientific message. The current practice of "balanced" reporting leads every scientific report of "an ice-berg to port" to be accompanied by a balancing report that "it has also been reported that the ice-berg is to starboard, or non-existent". There is a clear pattern by which the media give equal time to heavy-weight peer reviewed scientific findings, and remarks by industry-funded flacks.

- Joseph Romm has asked rhetorically: What is the reason for this flawed and incomplete reporting? To which he replies "One reason is that the Delayers have been hard at work criticizing the media for making the link between extreme weather and climate change – and they've succeeded in intimidating them. In his 2004 book, *Boiling Point*, Pulitzer Prize-winning journalist Ross Gelbspan wonders why journalists covering extreme weather events don't use the statement 'Scientists associated this pattern of violent weather with global warming.' He reports that a few years earlier he had asked 'a top editor in a major TV network' why they didn't make the link. The reply was: 'We did that. Once. But it triggered a barrage of complaints from the Global Climate Coalition [then the major anti-global-warming lobbying group of the fossil fuel industry] to our top executives at the network'."[127]

- There have been reports of NOAA (National Oceanic and Atmospheric Administration) refused a media interview with Thomas Knutson (on intensity of tropical storms related to global warming) in October 2006, and in February 2006 NASA tried to muzzle James Hansen their leading climate scientist. As NOAA policy a "minder" has to sit in on any interviews with the press.

Box 8: Coaching Instructions for Republicans on Global Warming

The complete text of the Luntz Companies advice to Republicans as to how to discuss environmental issues is available at: http://www.luntzspeak.com/graphics/LuntzResearch.Memo.pdf or in more abbreviated form in Annex 7.

The existence of this memo (that was written in 1999) was reported by Jennifer 8. Lee in the New York Times, in March, 2003[128], subsequently Mr. Luntz has said he would no longer give this advice[129], presumably since it is no longer plausible that there is any serious doubt about the existence of global warming (or "climate change" as Mr. Luntz would say, or "very adverse climate change" as the rest of us are experiencing it).

Basically Mr. Luntz's advice comes down to:

• Paint the Democrats as keen to regulate from Washington.

• Connect with the audience on a shared concern for the environment.

• Provide examples of bureaucratic failure to protect the environment.

• Describe personal examples of these concerns.

• Emphasize the need to balance environmental and economic concerns.

• Emphasize scientific uncertainty.

• And more.

Crucially readers are warned: *The scientific debate is closing [against us] but is not yet closed. There is still a window of opportunity to challenge the science.* And that once voters believe that there is a scientific basis for global warming, they will require action.

Politically, this advice was prescient, by 2003 republican candidates were faced with a President who had withdrawn from the Kyoto accord, and refused to accept the scientific consensus that global warming was real and man-made. Basically they had a choice on global warming, they could run against the President, or they could use the above types of argument to rationalize Republican policy.

Morally, this advice is indefensible. The only doubts by 1999 were voiced by people funded by the Global Climate Coalition, a group dedicated to confusing the public about global warming. There was no serious peer reviewed literature that doubted global warming. To ignore (or go against) scientific advice is to invite catastrophe. If half the effort that went into polling and focus groups to provide the above advice had gone into ascertaining the consensus of peer reviewed science, it would have been recognized that the scientific debate was already closed, and there was no responsible basis for business as usual.

We have lost four (or is it eight, or sixteen?) years in starting to respond to global warming due to the complete lack of statesmanship amongst our political leadership and their feckless consultants; dedicated simply to winning the next election, at no matter what cost to future generations.

- Since action (or rather inaction) on global warming has become a political issue, apologist Republicans have been extremely well briefed as to how to confuse the public, (Box 8).

- In June, 2005 the New York Times published an article, *Bush Aide Softened Greenhouse Gas Links to Global Warming,* which states that Philip A. Cooney, White House Council on Environmental Quality's chief of staff, formerly with the American Petroleum Institute, altered climate research already vetted by government scientists. What are we doing with someone from the American Petroleum Institute, altering reports on global warming? (See Box 10.)

- "For the last twenty years Earth scientists have concentrated on building predictive models of first the physical climate, followed by the integrated biogeochemistry of the planet. Unfortunately, these models operate implicitly as if humans did not exist. The new challenge is to build Earth Systems models that incorporate human policy options, economic preferences, and decision making that can then feed back to influence the biophysical states of the system. The increase in model complexity and interdisciplinary requirements is daunting."[132] Get that? Current models make no allowance for human decision making (aka elasticity of demand, or turning off a light switch), and as such cannot begin to consider the impact of alternative policies. (Pause and count to ten.)

Box 9: China Follows the Bush Doctrine

A recent article in Foreign Affairs[130] paints a disastrous picture of Chinese economy hell-bent on growth without regard to environmental damage. This is not attributed to any lack of central government concern for the environment, but that the central governments writ does not extend to how individual companies choose to expand, and local officials have few incentives to place a priority on environmental protection.

China is a coal-intensive economy. Coal provides about 70 percent of total energy, and is used inefficiently. Coal consumption looks set to double from 2000 to 2008. Even in 2006 China used more coal than the United States, United Kingdom and Japan combined. Value added per ton of coal is only one third of that in India, and one sixth of Japan's. There is no expectation of any early slow down in the rate of expansion, since Premier Wen has called for quadrupling the Chinese economy by 2020.

China is on another crash program: To equal the West in private mobility. Currently 14,000 new cars are sold each day, and over 50,000 miles of new roads are under construction. China expects to have 130 million cars by 2020 and more cars than the United States in 2050.

The U.K. Guardian[131] reports that "It is widely believed in economic circles that the country should focus on development first before cutting greenhouse gas emissions." This is the Bush Doctrine: *My approach recognizes that sustained economic growth is the solution, not the problem.*

Box 10: House Hearing on January 30, 2007.[133]

At a House hearing today lawmakers looked into allegations administration officials have been squeezing federal scientists studying climate change. Eric Niiler has more:

ERIC NIILER: A survey of 279 federal scientists found nearly half were pressured to drop references to global warming in their research. Study author Francesco Grifo of the Union of Concerned Scientists told the panel today that the changes amount to censorship.

FRANCESCO GRIFO: What we are calling for is that scientists are allowed to speak about their scientific results and get that information out to the taxpayers that are paying for it, to the community at large, to policymakers, to everyone that needs to really understand this issue.

Missouri Democrat William Lacy Clay said Administration officials have a clear agenda.

WILLIAM LACY CLAY: They have shown they would rather safeguard the interests of Big Oil than preserve the future of Planet Earth.

White House officials were not scheduled to speak today. They've refused to hand over documents the committee wants to see. President Bush has said he's concerned about global warming. But, he says, mandatory cuts of greenhouse gases would cost too much.

- "The WG2 Report calls for adopting a risk management perspective in assessing impacts, adaptation, and sustainable development. Indeed, risk-based portraits of impacts--net of the effects of alternative adaptations--can, when inserted into alternative development pathways at specific locations, offer decision-makers insight into climate risks calibrated in many different metrics (such as millions at risk of hunger or water stress in addition to economic damages)"[134]: Which is mechanistic and incomprehensible.

Box 11: Letter to NYTimes

Corporate Chiefs, Its Time to Go Green

To the Editor:

Re, "Auto Chiefs Make Headway Against Mileage Increase", (Business Day, June 7):

Anyone with a passing knowledge of the predicted impacts of global warming, and an ounce of common sense, should view with horror and disbelief the recent bullying push by Big Coal to lock the United States into generations of ever-growing, coal-based greenhouse gas emissions, and the latest refusal by the Big Three to make their automobiles significantly more fuel-efficient.

Do these corporate executives, and their well-supported political allies in Washington, really not understand what is at stake here? That we are fast approaching changes to the planet's physical, chemical and biological systems that will last for hundreds if not many thousands of years. That so long as the United States does little to cap its escalating emissions China and India will have no incentive to do so.

And that by their behavior, they are choosing potential profits over the health and the lives of not only my children and grandchildren and grand-grandchildren, but their own as well.

Eric Chivian, M.D.

Boston, June 8, 2007

The writer is director of the Center for Health and the Global Environment at Harvard University.

- "Adapting to the global climate change impacts outlined in the IPCC's Working Group 2 Report, 'Climate Change 2007: Impacts, Adaptation and Vulnerability', *will require new evaluation tools* to help choose the best way forward, according to the International Geosphere-Biosphere Program (IGBP), an international network of environmental scientists."[135] New evaluation tools? This is not encouraging!

It reveals that the IPCC's focus has been on climate change unrelated in any realistic way to human behavior, which has been taken as mechanistic or "exogenous". Only now are minds turning to what is really needed.

- Even from the technical climate modeling perspective, current models are deficient: They provide a linear description of a non-linear world. There are several known feed-back mechanisms that can lead to very sudden "burps" of carbon into the atmosphere[136], burning of the remaining Amazon, Congo and Indonesian forests, melting of the permafrost, volatilization of methane hydrate deposits in the polar oceans. These are not represented in current models because although we know they could occur, we lack empirically based hypotheses as what would trigger such "burps". The models seem to have a good handle on how long it will take for Greenland and Antarctic ice to melt, but no provision is made for the catastrophic effects on sea level should the ice-sheets continue to accelerate to the point that they *slip into the ocean* before melting.

- The key message provided by the modeling industry is that it is imperative that we take "immediate action" (i.e. within the next decade) lest we face terrible outcomes in 2100, such as a 4 degree centigrade rise in temperature, and up to a meter rise in sea level. *The result is to suggest that we have plenty of time (a decade or so), and in any case the problem we are seeking to avoid is not that dire.*

- The Speaker of the House, Nancy Pelosi has announced a target of making House operations carbon neutral by the end of this session of Congress, while Senator John Kerry has drafted legislation to make the whole Capitol complex carbon neutral by 2020... An initial step has been to have House workers replace 2,000 incandescent bulbs with compact florescent lamps (CFLs), the remaining 10,000 to be replaced by December 2007[137]. When the Congress starts changing the light bulbs, you just know you are on the Titanic! "Carbon neutral" should be a warning, see Chapter

155

4, they are planning to use carbon credits to achieve carbon neutrality. But most importantly, *the Congress seems not to realize that their job is not to ensure that the Capitol Complex does not AFCO2TA, but that the whole country does not AFCO2TA!* Better that the whole world cease AFCO2TA.

- At the same time the Congressional leadership is planning to make at least the Capitol complex carbon neutral, the Senate has a draft Bill to provide $10 billion of loans for liquid-coal plants with sequestration, which would still increase slightly the emissions compared to the gasoline[138] (see Table 5).

- Scientists see their role as the provision of (conservative) "objective factually based evidence", and to leave *policy* formation to politicians and their advisors. The result of this *conservative* advice is that repeatedly anticipated phenomena occur, but much earlier than they are expected. .... "From 2000 to 2004, emissions grew at a rate of three percent a year- more than the highest rate used in a recent UN (IPCC) report"[139]

- The Stern Review, rightly reflected the consensus of climate scientists: "The lesson is to avoid doing too much, too fast". Meanwhile Richard Alley said in May 2006, (i.e. well before the Stern Review came out): "The ice sheets seem to be shrinking 100 years ahead of schedule"[140].

In short there is little recognition in the Congress that global warming is a real phenomenon which needs to be dealt with radically, and immediately.

On Spaceship Titanic the crew are offering advice, but they consistently underestimate the risks we face, and even these warnings are muffled by the media's persistent deference to lobbying and the reporting of unqualified critics. Dr. Hansen's testimony, reviewed at length in Chapter 13, stands out as a model of what scientists and experts could and should be providing by way of guidance on global warming.

But what of the passengers?

- The passengers are "conflicted" as the young folk say. On the one hand everyday, casual observation reveals that the weather is getting warmer. On the other hand, who is to complain about a shorter winter? And a longer hotter summer is easily combated by running the air conditioner a little longer. *For many people global warming, as currently experienced, is not unpleasant.*

- But what about Katrina? Well that was way down south in New Orleans. What about extended forest fires? Well that is mostly way out west in Colorado, Wyoming or California. What about a whole town flattened by a tornado in Kansas? Well, that was in Kansas. I mean, right here in River City, we have had no serious adverse effects.

- About half the leading environmental organizations still do not recognize global warming as the primordial problem. If environmentalists don't give global warming top priority, what chance is there for the less environmentally aware to recognize the problem? The Environmental Defense Fund in particular takes credit for fostering USCAP an energy company sponsored coalition to promote C&T. Where *elimination* of AFCO2TA is simply not on the agenda. Successful elimination of AFCO2TA, implies ceasing to use coal, implies that large coal companies, such as Peabody coal, will need to close, or find a new line of business.

- Yes storing nuclear waste may make part of the planet uninhabitable for hundreds of thousands of years, but continuing to use fossil fuels risks making the planet as a whole uninhabitable for millions of years.

- The World Watch Institute and the Natural Resources Defense Council are reported as saying that there are "a lot better carbon-free alternatives". It is irresponsible to oppose nuclear without specifying what these alternatives are and how our energy needs are to be met.

- There are at least 200 nimby type wind farm opposition groups in the U.S., and many more in other developed countries. This indicates ignorance in depth of the damage global warming is doing, or a beggar-my-neighbor attitude that somebody else can pay the costs of dispensing with fossil fuels.

- Deep down many people agree with the President that "technology will dig us out of this". There is no appreciation that the technologies being primarily supported by government (clean coal, liquid-coal, hydrogen and ethanol) have no chance of replacing fossil fuels in a timely fashion, and are quite likely to increase AFCO2TA.

- Even those concerned with global warming are focused on: How we will deal with global warming? When the real question is: How will global warming deal with us?

- People have been lulled by the idea that we have a decade to make difficult decisions. Whereas these are the same difficult decisions that we should have made fifteen years ago.

- There is absolutely no understanding that the simple turning on of an electric light contributes to priming (climatic) Weapons of Mass Destruction way beyond anything consciously created by man.

- How could a great modern ship like the Titanic possibly be damaged by a bit of ice?

- Like the Titanic, it seems that it will not be until the disaster is fully upon us, and irreversible, that people will realize that there are not enough lifeboats to go round.

If any optimists remain who believe that "the government would never allow us to destroy our planet", a brief reading of *Collapse* by Jaret Diamond would be salutary: Both the Vikings in Eastern Greenland, and Easter Islanders failed to modify their life-styles. To the point where the Vikings died out, and Easter Islanders who used to trade across the Pacific, cut down their last tree and dropped to a subsistence economy with a fraction of their former population.

Truly the most worrying thing about global warming is that neither the President, nor the Congress nor the people really believe that it is a serious problem.

And yet, after this full recital of all the ills of climate change that emerge from Pandora's Box, there is also a hope. Congressman John Dingell, Chairman of the House Energy and Commerce Committee has recently introduced draft legislation providing carbon tax of $10 a ton, rising over 5 years to a tax of $50 per ton. Some of the resulting revenue would be used to increase the earned income tax credit, and the balance for good causes such as Medicare and Social Security, Universal Healthcare (when passed), research on Renewable Energy and the like. Much more modest than the policy proposals put forward in this book, the draft proposals are nevertheless headed in the right direction. Congressman Dingell's target is a 60 to 80% reduction in carbon emissions by 2050, clearly indicating that the problem is not yet seen as immediate or drastic. Worse, he is working on a parallel C&T proposal. Nevertheless he is clearly open to new energy policies, and has got the basic message that the price of fossil carbon has to be raised for global warming to be affected.

Chapter 15: Keeping Tabs

Since thousands of scientists (mostly with Ph.Ds) are involved in the production of the IPCC reports, it might appear impossible for the average citizen to keep tabs on how our global warming policies are working. It turns out however, that there is no difficulty in keeping tabs on the concentration of ACO2, that is the major driving force for global warming. This data is recorded by NOAA at the Moana Loa observatory in Hawaii.

To get the most recent readings from Moana Loa it is only necessary to:

i)   Google "moana loa CO2", and click on "Trends in Carbon Dioxide". Alternatively you can go directly to www.esrl. noaa.gov/gmd/ccgg/trends/. Half way down the page you will see: Click here for the Mauna Loa CO2 monthly mean data.

ii) Click on , Mauna Loa CO2 monthly mean data. This gives a listing on Notepad, as a continuous stream of data.

iii) Go to the Notepad "tool bar" at the top, and click on "Format", this gives a drop-down menu, click on "Word Wrap". This should give the data in an easily read form, as below:

MLO	2005	01	378.43	MLO	2005	02	379.70	MLO	2005	03	380.92
MLO	2005	04	382.18	MLO	2005	05	382.45	MLO	2005	06	382.14
MLO	2005	07	380.60	MLO	2005	08	378.64	MLO	2005	09	376.73
MLO	2005	10	376.84	MLO	2005	11	378.29	MLO	2005	12	380.06
MLO	2006	01	381.40	MLO	2006	02	382.20	MLO	2006	03	382.66
MLO	2006	04	384.69	MLO	2006	05	384.94	MLO	2006	06	384.01
MLO	2006	07	382.14	MLO	2006	08	380.31	MLO	2006	09	378.81
MLO	2006	10	379.03	MLO	2006	11	380.17	MLO	2006	12	381.85
MLO	2007	01	382.94	MLO	2007	02	383.86	MLO	2007	03	384.49
MLO	2007	04	386.37	MLO	2007	05	386.54	MLO	2007	06	385.98
MLO	2007	07	384.35	MLO	2007	08	381.91				

iv) If you "copy" a relevant section of the table and "paste" it into a word document it will appear as a column:

....

MLO	2006	11	380.17
MLO	2006	12	381.85
MLO	2007	01	382.94
MLO	2007	02	383.86
MLO	2007	03	384.49
MLO	2007	04	386.37
MLO	2007	05	386.54
MLO	2007	06	385.98
MLO	2007	07	384.35
MLO	2007	08	381.91

v) It is then a simple matter to rearrange the data (atmospheric carbon in ppm) manually as:

	2005	2006	2007	2006-2005	2007-2006
1 Jan	378.43	381.40	382.94	2.97	1.54
2 Feb	379.70	382.20	383.86	2.50	1.66
3 Mar	380.92	382.66	384.49	1.74	1.83
4 Apr	382.18	384.69	386.37	2.51	1.68
5 May	382.45	384.94	386.54	2.49	1.60
6 Jun	382.14	384.01	385.98	1.87	1.97
7 Jul	380.60	382.14	384.35	1.54	2.21
8 Aug	378.64	380.31	381.91	1.67	1.60
9 Sep	376.73	378.81		2.08	
10 Oct	376.84	379.03		2.19	
11 Nov	378.29	380.17		1.88	
12 Dec	380.06	381.85		1.79	
Average				2.10	

We are now ready to "keep tabs", which we do by adding the two right-hand difference columns above.

Looking at the above figures for 2005, 2006 and 2007 we can see that the maximum ACO2 concentration within the year occurs in May, and the low point in September. From September to May there is a slow build up of ACO2, in part due to AFCO2TA, and in part due to bio-carbon sequestered in plants, rotting, or being eaten or burned and returned to the atmosphere. From May to September there is a relatively fast decline in ACO2, as plant growth in the northern hemisphere withdraws CO2 from the atmosphere faster than CO2 is returned from sequestered bio-carbon plus net additions of fossil carbon.

As we look at the concentration of ACO2 for the same month in successive years we can see that there is a steady increase. The amount of the increase varies between years and months, but is consistently positive. Between 2005 and 2006 the average increase was 2.10, meaning that on average the ACO2 was 2.10 ppm higher in 2006 than in 2005. Comparing the rate of increase from 2005 to 2006, with the increase from 2006 to 2007, it looks as if the rate of increase is falling. If this is true, it is excellent news.

However, there are no policy changes that seem likely to explain the slow-down in the *rate of increase*, nor was there a significant drop in economic activity in the first half of 2007. In any case, while an increase of "only" 1.54 ppm from January 2006 to January 2007 is clearly better than the increase of 2.97 ppm from January 2005 to January 2006, we will not be able to "breath easy" *until the year to year increase has dropped to zero.*

Access to the Moana Loa data allows us to monitor the progress (or lack of progress) in combating global warming month by month.

Using this same data series, and a simple statistical technique known as regression, we can look forward and see ACO2 is likely to increase, if no policy changes are made ("business as usual", BAU).

This also gives us a bench mark against which we can measure the overall impact of policy changes on the level of ACO2.

Looking back at Figure 5, we can see that for any given month the concentration of ACO2 in ppm (parts per million) is a smoothly rising curve. Month by month, it is possible to estimate (by regression) the form this curve takes as a function of time (years). If we fit a straight line we can explain about 98.71 percent of the variation shown in Figure 5. If we fit a quadratic we get to explain 99.89%, and a cubic we explain 99.90%. (These actual figures are for December, but other months are similar.)

These regression estimates, based on past observations, can be used to estimate/predict/project future ACO2 concentrations. This has been done below (Table 8) for each month through 2010, and for 2015, and 2020. Clearly actual observed concentrations will differ from the projections, but these differences will tell us a story. Moreover in another year, the data from 2007 can be incorporated into the regressions, which will likely lead to a slight revision of the numerical estimates.

Actual concentrations are available for the first nine months of 2007, and are shown. The difference between actual observation and the quadratic estimate is also shown. All but one of these differences (actual less projection) are positive (0.22, 0.25, 0.14, 0.50, 0.36, 0.36, 0.39, -0.11, 0.13) indicating that actual ACO2 concentrations are *higher* than would have been projected on the basis of historical rates of increase in ACO2.

Comparisons have been made to the quadratic function (rather than the cubic) since the predictive power is almost the same, and the quadratic is closer to the actual in 2007. (Readers are welcome to use the cubic, or linear, results should they so wish).

Two things to note:

- For the first nine months of 2007, actual ACO2 concentration has been way above the linear and cubic estimates, and above the quadratic in seven of nine months. For the moment however, actual ACO2 concentrations seem to be marking out a new higher path.

- In any case, the rise in ACO2 is not due only to poor American policy, or indeed poor policy from the developed countries, it reflect poor policies world wide. It is likely that the rapid expansion of coal based power stations in China and to a lesser extent India are contributing to the apparent acceleration in the rate of adding FCO2TA, and that drought induced forest fires in the U.S. and elsewhere are contributing to shifting carbon within the carbon cycle from sequestered trees to ACO2. These are development not properly reflected in the historical data series.

The following tables have space to enter actual ACO2 levels as they become known, and to insert notes on major global warming events (both weather and policy related).

If you send me an email at wcandler1@comcast.net, with the word "Update" in the title, I will send you an annual update of more recent projections based on all actual observed data to date (and colored versions of the figures in the book).

The formulas used to get the January estimates are:

<u>Linear</u>:

ppm(Jan) = 308.87322 + 1.41440*Y

<u>Quadratic</u>:

ppm(Jan) = 314.00873 + 0.80598*Y + 0.01217*Y*Y

<u>Cubic</u>:

ppm(Jan) = 314.68008 + 0.65356*Y + 0.01976*Y*Y
$$- 0.00010*Y*Y*Y$$

where Y = Year − 1958.

1958 is the first year in which Moana Loa was recorded. Thus for a quadratic trend estimate of ppm in 2050 we would get:

ppm(Jan) = 314.00873 + 0.80598*92 + 0.01217*92*92
          = 491.16

Just because we can forecast these ACO2 concentrations does not mean that the associated weather patterns will be acceptable, and while stopping using fossil fuels would stop AFCO2TA, it is not necessary that this would stop a rise in ACO2, due to feed-back loops triggered by higher temperatures, that could shift massive amounts of bio-carbon *within* the carbon cycle.

We cannot expect climate to stabilize again until there is *no expected change* in ppm of CO2 from year to year, for a given month.

Dr. Hansen associates a 1o Centigrade temperature rise (from 2000) or 450 ppm of ACO2 with tipping points. Using our simple-Johnny regressions, we can say that under business as usual the current projections for when this concentration would be reached is:

2058 if the linear expression is used,

2036 if the quadratic expression is used, and

2042 if the cubic expression is used.

To the extent that actual ACO2 concentrations prove to lie above the estimated levels in Table 8, we can expect the 450 ppm level to be reached earlier, to the extent that policies result in actual concentrations below the projections we can expect the arrival of the 450 ppm level to be delayed.

As individual citizens we are in a position to monitor how successfully global warming is being abated.

It cannot be too strongly emphasized that to avoid reaching the 450 ppm level *we would have to stop AFCO2TA long before these dates*, as feed-back loops within the carbon cycle will almost certainly shift sequestered carbon within the cycle into the atmosphere, in response to higher temperatures.

Since stopping AFCO2TA means no coal, no oil, no natural gas, no cement/concrete, and certainly no tar sands or methane hydrate, the required transformation is mind boggling. *Clearly the time for serious policy changes is NOW.*

Table 8.1   Monthly Projected Atmospheric CO2 Concentrations, 2007

2007 Month	Linear	Quadratic	Cubic	Actual	Diff
Jan	378.14	382.72	382.19	382.94	0.22
Feb	379.01	383.61	383.	383.86	0.25
Mar	379.76	384.35	383.86	384.49	0.14
Apr	381.12	385.87	385.45	386.37	0.50
May	381.55	386.18	385.62	386.54	0.36 .
Remark: *Heavy Floods in York, U.K*				385.98	0.36
Jun	380.98	385.62	385.09		

Remark: *Wildfires in West, U.S.A., Flooding in Japan, Congress to change light bulbs. Heavy Flooding in Gloster, U.K.*

Jul	379.26	383.96	383.46	384.35	0.39
Aug	377.17	382.02	381.54	381.91	-0.11
Sep	375.12	380.45	379.71	380.55	0.13
Oct	375.40	380.64	379.80		

Remark: *500,000 people evacuated from California wild fires. Acute drought in southern U.S. (Atlanta within 90 days of running out of water.)*

Nov	376.88	382.09	381.37
Dec	378.43	383.61	382.94

Table 8.2 Monthly Projected Atmospheric CO2 Concentrations, 2008

2008 Month	Linear	Quadratic	Cubic	Actual	Diff	Remark
Jan	379.56	384.73	384.06			
Feb	380.43	385.62	384.98			
Mar	381.16	386.35	385.72			
Apr	382.53	387.89	387.36			
May	382.96	388.18	387.47			
Jun	382.39	387.62	386.95			
Jul	380.66	385.96	385.33			
Aug	378.56	384.04	383.42			
Sep	376.50	382.48	381.56			
Oct	376.79	382.66	381.61			
Nov	378.28	384.12	383.22			
Dec	379.84	385.64	384.81			

Table 8.3 Monthly Projected Atmospheric CO2 Concentrations, 2009

2009 Month	Linear	Quadratic	Cubic	Actual	Diff	Remark
Jan	380.97	386.76	385.93			
Feb	381.84	387.67	386.86			
Mar	382.57	388.37	387.58			
Apr	383.95	389.94	389.27			
May	384.37	390.21	389.33			
Jun	383.80	389.65	388.82			
Jul	382.06	387.98	387.20			
Aug	379.96	386.08	385.31			
Sep	377.88	384.52	383.41			
Oct	378.19	384.71	383.43			
Nov	379.68	386.17	385.08			
Dec	381.25	387.70	386.69			

Table 8.4 Monthly Projected Atmospheric CO2 Concentrations, 2010

2010 Month	Linear	Quadratic	Cubic	Actual	Diff	Remark
Jan	382.39	388.82	387.81			
Feb	383.26	389.73	388.76			
Mar	383.98	390.41	389.46			
Apr	385.36	392.01	391.20			
May	385.78	392.26	391.20			
Jun	385.21	391.70	390.70			
Jul	383.45	390.03	389.09			
Aug	381.35	388.14	387.21			
Sep	379.26	386.59	385.26			
Oct	379.58	386.78	385.26			
Nov	381.08	388.25	386.95			
Dec	382.66	389.78	388.57			

Table 8.5 Monthly Projected Atmospheric CO2 Concentrations, 2015

2015 Month	Linear	Quadratic	Cubic	Actual	Diff	Remark
Jan	389.46	399.48	397.33			
Feb	390.35	400.43	398.35			
Mar	391.03	400.97	398.98			
Apr	392.43	402.72	401.02			
May	392.83	402.85	400.62			
Jun	392.25	402.29	400.18			
Jul	390.45	400.62	398.63			
Aug	388.32	398.83	396.87			
Sep	386.17	397.32	394.63			
Oct	386.53	397.49	394.42			
Nov	388.08	398.99	396.36			
Dec	389.71	400.55	398.10			

Table 8.6 Monthly Projected Atmospheric CO2 Concentrations, 2020

2020 Month	Linear	Quadratic	Cubic	Actual	Diff	Remark
Jan	396.53	410.75	406.97			
Feb	397.44	411.74	408.09			
Mar	398.07	412.12	408.63			
Apr	399.50	414.03	411.06			
May	399.88	414.04	410.13			
Jun	399.30	413.48	409.79			
Jul	397.44	411.81	408.34			
Aug	395.29	410.13	406.72			
Sep	393.07	408.68	404.07			
Oct	393.49	408.83	403.56			
Nov	395.08	410.35	405.84			
Dec	396.76	411.93	407.74			

Annex 1: Carbon Credit Suppliers May, 2007.

How much does Carbon Offsetting cost? Price survey![141]

Example: a mid-sized 30 mpg car driving 12,000 miles/year will create about 3.55 tons of CO2/year. Using Carbonfund.org's calculator we figured this would cost only about $19.50 or $1.63/month to be offset! **This means that for a very small amount of money you can drive the equivalent of a zero-CO2-emission car!**

It is up to each of us to clean our own mess, obviously the government can't and won't do it (alone). Signing up with any of these programs might effectively reduce your CO2 contributions to ZERO! (All prices in US$)

Ecobusinesslinks.com Carbon Offset Survey

Carbon Offset Provider	Price (US$/ Metric ton CO2)	Non-profit	Projects Types	Project Choice	Offset Types	Product Certification/ Verification
AtmosClear Climate Club						
US	$3.56a - $25.00	No	Methane	No	Car, Home	Environmental Resources Trust
Carbonfund.org						
US	$4.30b - 5.50	Yes	Renewables, Efficiency, Reforestation	Yes	Home, Car, Air, Events, Business	Green-e, Chicago Climate Exchange, Environmental Resources Trust
e-BlueHorizons						

US	$5.00	No	Renewables, Reforestation	No	Home, Car, Air	Chicago Climate Exchange, Environmental Resources Trust
DriveNeutral.org						
US	$6.93 & up	Yes	Efficiency	No	Car	Chicago Climate Exchange
Terrapass						
US	$7.35c – 11.00	No	Renewables, Efficiency	No	Car, Air, Events, Business	Green-e, Chicago Climate Exchange, Center for Resource Solutions
DrivingGreen						
Ireland	$8.00	No	Renewables	No	Car, Air, Events	SES
Native Energy						
US	$13.20	No	Renewables	Yes	Home, Car, Air, Events, Business	Green-e
The CarbonNeutral Company						
UK	$14.00-18.00	No	Renewables, Efficiency, Reforestation,			

Company	Country	Price	Gold Standard	Type	Additional	Coverage	Verified by
Methane			Yes			Business, Home, Car, Air, Events	KPMG, Edinburgh Centre for Carbon Management, Independent Advisory Committee
Climate Friendly	Australia	$16.00-19.00	No	Renewables	No	Home, Car, Air, Business	Office of the Renewable Energy Regulator, NSW Government, Ernst & Young.
Sustainable travel International	US, Switzerland	$18.00	Yes	Renewables	No	Air, Car, Home, Hotel	See Myclimate
Uncook the Planet	Australia	$19.45	No	Efficiency	No	Air, Car, Home, Business	Greenhouse Gas Abatement Scheme Project
Bonneville Environmental Foundation	US	$29.00	Yes	Renewables	No	Home, Air, Business, Event	Green-e
Global Cool	UK	£20.00					

Carbon Offset Provider	Price (US$/ Metric ton CO2)	Verification	Projects Types	Project Choice	Offset Types	Product Certification/ Designated Operational Entity
Myclimate, Switzerland ($39.48)	$53.00	Yes	Renewables	Yes	Air, Events, Business	CDM
Services for which we couldn't find independent product certification or verification information		Non-profit	No	n/a		n/a
Solar Electric Light Fund, US	$10.00	Yes	Renewables	No	External	n/a
Carbon Clear, UK	$14.48	No	Reforestation	No	Home, Car, Air, Babies	n/a

a: Atmos Clear - Low price for 25 Ton option at $89

b: Carbonfund.org - Low price for ZeroCarbon tags option: 18 Ton + 5 Ton match, pay $99 for $23 Ton

c: Terrapass - Low price when purchasing 204 metric ton of carbon offsets for $1,499.95

1. Offset Types: There are hundreds of potential offset types. We have limited our survey to just the most common.

2. Verification: "n/a" means we were unable to determine a third-party verification body. The projects may, however, be verified.

3. Choice: refers to whether customers may choose between project types and/or specific projects.

4. Price: prices change and exchange rates fluctuate. The data listed was first gathered from the respective websites July 21, 2006

5. Other offset providers may exist. This survey provides a cross section of the industry, projects may be added or removed over time.

6. Some information may be incomplete or has changed. We welcome updates.

Annex 2: Environmental Resource Trust: Project Verification Statement

Participant Data

Name: **Inland Empire Utility Agency (IEUA)**

Contacts: **Richard Atwater**

Prepared by: **Wiley Barbour, ERT**

Emissions Model **IEUA Digester Model 2004 – 012406 (excel spreadsheet)**

MRV Protocol: **Inland MRV Protocol 01-24-2006 (word document)**

Summary

Based on its review, ERT has verified the information submitted by IEUA as being consistent with the attached monitoring, reporting, and verification protocol. ERT has registered a total of 8,008 metric tons of CO_2 equivalent emission reductions in 2003 and 5,893 tons of CO_2-e reductions in 2004, conditioned on the following findings and adjustments.

Key Findings*

Project Boundaries & Dates:

The project boundaries are consistent with those described in the MRV Protocol. The project dates associated with the emission reductions verified in this statement are 1 January 2003 through 31 December 2004.

Additionality & Leakage:

The emission reductions were verified to be additional, given existing regulatory requirements. No leakage of emissions outside the project boundaries was identified.

Baseline: The baseline is unmitigated release of *all air pollutants*[142], both from the local dairies where manure was stockpiled and stored in lagoons, and from agricultural fields where manure was land applied.

Monitoring, Data Collection, & Methodology:

In general, procedures were in keeping with the MRV protocol. The following deviations were determined to be acceptable.

Measurements of biogas characteristics (composition, methane content, sulfur content, heat content) are taken sporadically by IEUA and contractors. A more systematic and regular testing procedure would enhance data quality.

Incoming honey vacs and transfer containers delivering manure to the digester are weighed on a tipping scale at RP-5. Also, measurements of total solids and volatile solids are taken at RP-5. There is no scale at RP-1 requiring an estimation of weight based on the assumption that density is identical to loads received at RP-5. Although this is likely to be an accurate assumption a scale at RP-1 would enhance data quality. Measurements of TS and VS at RP-1 are taken after water is added to achieve desired dilution. This invalidates the data for use in the baseline calculations, requiring an assumption that solids content of undiluted loads at RP-1 have identical TS and VS properties as manure received at RP-5. Again, this is unlikely to cause a bias in the data. The efficiency of methane destruction in the flare was based on typical flare manufacturer's guaranteed value of 98 percent, which is also supported by the default value in EPA's AP-42 volume.

Quality Control, Reporting, Documentation, & Uncertainties:
Quality control, reporting, and documentation procedures followed were in keeping with the MRV protocol. Although the methane content measurements were only taken sporadically, relatively low variability was observed between measurements.

Incremental Account Adjustment
Valid as of: **24 January 2006**
Registered reductions (metric tons of CO_2-equivalents): **5,893**
Vintage Year(s): **2004**
ERT Serial Numbers:

Page 3 of 3 Version 2004.1
Attachments/Exhibits Special Notes
Note that the registration of the project reduction at IEUA is performed in the context of ongoing efforts at IEUA to complete a corporate-wide inventory and register entity wide emissions with ERT.

Disclaimer: While ERT believes that all allocations in its GHG Registry® result from a true and fair representation of participants' emissions performance, ERT assumes no liability for the allocations in the GHG Registry® or the uses to which they are put. Use of the GHG Registry® is governed under the terms and conditions of the GHG Registry® user agreement.

Environmental Resoures Trust, Inc.
1612 K St., NW Suite 1400
Washington, D.C. 2006
Tel: 202 785 8577
Fax: 785 2739
www.ert.net
www.ecoregistry.org

Annex 3: Offsets and "Future Value Accounting"

Jamie Hartzell

(Annex 1 of "The Carbon Neutral Myth: Indulgences for your Climate Sins").

Transnational Institute

De Wittenstraat 25

1052 AK Amsterdam

The Netherlands

www.carbontradewatch.org

www.tni.org

First Published February, 2007: ISBN 9789071007187)

We often hear offset companies talking about how we can offset our personal emissions. But what is the main aim of offsetting? It is to reduce our carbon emissions to zero.

The Carbon Neutral Company calls this being carbon neutral. Climate Care says we can be climate neutral. But if you look at the websites of Climate Care or the Carbon Neutral Company you won't find the terms carbon neutral or climate neutral defined. They leave that to our intuition. So what do we think these terms actually mean?

We can say then that intuitively carbon or climate neutral means that the same amount of carbon that we cause to emit is offset through carbon reduction or absorption projects such as tree planting, energy efficiency or renewable energy generation projects. We could say that our carbon emissions and our carbon offsets are 'in balance'. Our carbon budget, or our carbon balance, is zero.

But this definition ignores one key question: over what time frame does the amount of carbon emitted have to be fully offset for our carbon balance to be zero?

Let me present a few possible views on the acceptability of different time frames:

1. The life of a tree is 100 years, so I am happy if my emissions are offset in that time frame

2. I'd want to see all my emissions offset in 20 years, by 2026

3. My emissions should be reduced by 20 per cent by 2012, in line with UK government targets

4. All my emissions should be offset within one year

5. All my emissions should be offset before the next time I fly

6. If it takes 5 hours to fly London New York, my emissions should be offset by the time I arrive.

Which of these are acceptable? And which would still legitimately allow the use of the term carbon neutral? To say that emissions have to be offset before a plane lands seems quite extreme. But equally, to take 100 years to offset our emissions does not seem acceptable, when global temperatures are set to rise several degrees and a large percentage of the world will be underwater in that time.

In fact, the speed with which we need to offset our emissions depends on two things:

First it depends on the impending nature of the climate crisis. Just how fast do we need to reduce our emissions to stop global warming?

Second, it depends on the rate at which global carbon dioxide emissions continue to rise. If emissions continue to go up, we need to offset even faster to meet reduction targets.

Plowing through the websites of the different offset companies, it is virtually impossible to see how they are treating the time issue. They

179

are clearly making assumptions about how many years the carbon saved will operate over, and so how much carbon will in the end be saved, but these assumptions are not published.

Climate Care offers three ways to offset your emissions - through energy efficiency projects, which make up 50 per cent of total carbon savings, renewable energy projects, which give 20 per cent of carbon savings, and tree planting, which gives the remaining 30 per cent.

From information gleaned from the annual report and website and through conversations with Tom Hinton, MD of Climate Care, I estimate that Climate Care calculates its emission reductions over approximately the following periods:

Table 3.1 Types of Project Used to Generate Offsets

Type of Project	Years to Offset Emmissions	Basis for Life of calculation	% of all offsets
Energy Efficiency	6	Low energy light bulb	50
Renewable Energy	12	Wind turbine	20
Tree Planting	100	Tree	30

With this information it is possible to calculate how long it takes to offset carbon through Climate Care. Let's take an example.

Say I flew to New York one way, on New Year's Eve 2005. According to Climate Care, this will result in the emission of 0.77 tonnes of carbon dioxide, which I can offset for £5.77, with the money I give them being spent on the range of projects listed above.

Over time, my carbon balance will then look like this:

You can see that by 2018, 12 years after I took the flight, my original emissions are 80 per cent offset. Six years of energy efficiency savings and 12 years of renewable energy generation are having their effect. But then things don't look so good. Because the tree projects are only offsetting my emissions at the rate of 0.3 per cent of my original emissions a year, it actually takes till 2106 before my emissions are completely neutralized. That's 100 years. What will be the state of the climate crisis by then?

But of course Climate Care isn't just claiming you can offset one flight and still be climate neutral. Their idea is that even if you fly every year, so long as you offset you will remain climate neutral. How true is this? Let's assume that I fly to New York and back again, every New Year's Eve for the next 30 years, and faithfully pay my £5.77 each time.

Using the same basis of calculation, my carbon budget now looks like this:

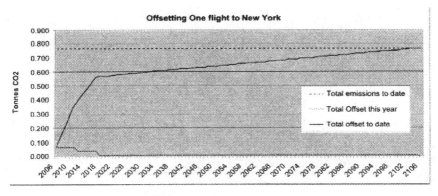

Figure 3.1 Offsetting One Flight to New York

Of course as I fly every year, my total emissions are steadily rising year on year, as shown by the top line. As I pay money to Climate Care every year, my offsets are also rising, as shown by the solid line. But my offsets are not rising as fast as my emissions, as they occur over a much longer time frame. And so, as the fine dotted line shows, my total emissions not offset are rising.

So not only is my position far from climate neutral, quite the opposite is true. Each time I fly, the carbon in the atmosphere increases. My carbon balance is going in the wrong direction.

Let's say I am a more frequent flyer. I take not one but three return flights to New York a year for 30 years. Is it harder for me to offset my emissions? Assuming I pay the £5.77 per flight Climate Care asks of me, my carbon balance then looks like this:

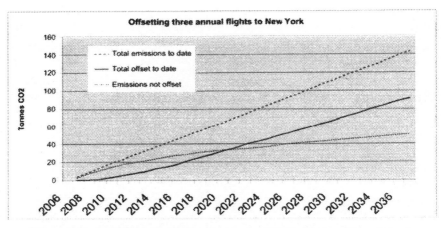

Figure 3.2 Offsetting Three Annual Flights to New York

The pattern is much the same, but the numbers are bigger. When I flew only once a year, by 2036 I was left with a 'negative balance' of 8.5 tonnes of CO2 that I hadn't managed to offset. When I fly six times as often, by 2036 I'm left with a staggering 51 tonnes of CO2 that I haven't offset. In each case that is 11 years of emissions that haven't been offset.

But the point is that when I fly more often, I am even less climate neutral. Flying more frequently means that I need to do more offsetting to have any hope of achieving climate neutrality.

So the idea of achieving climate neutrality through offsetting is no more than media spin. First, it takes 100 years to fully cancel out the carbon effect of one aeroplane flight. Second, the more you fly, the more you need to offset, and finally, depending on how quickly you think offsetting needs to happen, it is also more expensive to offset than Climate Care would lead us to believe.

How much should we be paying to offset? Let's go back to the original table of offset time objectives. How much should we be paying to Climate Care if we want to achieve our objectives:

Table 3.2 Cost of Carbon Offset as a Function of Time to Complete

Timespan to offset emissions in 100 years (Life span of tree)	Cost of offsetting a flight to New York £5.77
In 20 years, by 2026	£10
20% reduction by 2010, in accordance UK Government targets	£20
Within one year	£50
Before 1 fly again (3 flights a year)	£200
By the time my flight arrives	£86,402

So what can we conclude?

First, we are told that offsetting makes us climate neutral when it doesn't. Each time we fly, our emissions go up.

Second, offsetting is far too cheap. Depending on how quickly we think we need to offset, we need to be paying as much as 15,000 times more to see our emissions offset in a sensible time frame. The question remains if a company like Climate Care could even develop schemes fast enough to achieve this level of offsetting.

In a recent *New Internationalist* article, the founder of Climate Care Mike Mason was quoted as saying "I would rather that 100 per cent of people offset their emissions from flights than 50 per cent of those people not fly at all."

But if this were to happen, by Climate Care's own calculations, it would be 2020 before offsetting was achieving the same level of saving as a straight 50 per cent cut in flights. It's up to Mike to decide if he is willing to wait that long.

The reason why the offset companies can argue for carbon neutrality is they are using a carbon calculation method that is best termed 'future value accounting'. Carbon savings expected to be made in the future are counted as savings made in the present. This is the same technique used by Enron to inflate its profits - and sooner or later I expect, just like Enron, the house of cards will come tumbling down.

However I fear the technique of using "future value carbon accounting" may run much deeper than just the small schemes run by voluntary offset companies.

They may also apply to the Clean Development Mechanism of the Kyoto Protocol. This is the mechanism by which developed nations invest in the less developed to achieve future carbon savings, allowing them to then emit more carbon themselves.

The UK is looking to achieve two thirds of its carbon emissions reductions through this mechanism. But if this is done through 'future value carbon accounting', it will not be just a few carbon offset companies that come crashing down, it will be international climate negotiations.

Annex 4. Audit Report on Tradable Renewable Certificates (Carbon Credits)

October 20, 2006
Mr. Eric M. Carlson
Executive Director
Carbonfund.org
10001 Dallas Avenue
Silver Spring, MD 20901

Re: Green-e Annual Process Audit – Attest Engagement Agreed Upon Procedures Report

Dear Mr. Carlson:

From our engagement to perform the applicable procedures under the Center for Resource Solutions' (CRS) Green-e TRC Annual Process Audit Protocol ("CRS Protocol"), for the Green-e Tradable Renewable Certificates ("TRCs") Certification Program ("Green-e Program") for the year ended December 31, 2004 for Carbondfund.org, we issued a report dated October 9, 2006 and noted the following:

- Carbonfund.org received carbon offset donations for 2004 to purchase and retire 625 MWh of TRCs.

- Carbonfund.org purchased 625 MWh of 2004 eligible Green-e certified Wind TRCs from a Green-e certified wholesale product. The purchase was agreed to in the "Green-e Attestation from Wholesale Provider of Electricity or TRCs", which was provided by 3 Phases Energy Company, the wholesale provider of the Greene certified TRCs, to Carbonfund.org.

- The 625 MWh of 2004 eligible Green-e certified Wind TRCs were generated by the Rosebud Sioux Wind Project, based in Rosebud, South Dakota.

Based on the information above, we determined that Carbonfund.org purchased and retired 625 MWh of Green-e certified Wind TRCs to offset donations representing 625 MWh.

Sincerely,
W. David Rook
Officer/Shareholder
(713) 297-6903

Annex 5: Estimation of Carbon Tax Rates

This annex suggests a *procedure* for estimating carbon tax rates. Emphasis is on the proposed procedure or methodology. Numbers should be taken as representative, but will need to be tailored to the desired impact of the tax, current prices and cost structures, and updated technical specifications of the fossil fuels to be taxed.

Calculations are based, based on Energy Information Agency (EIA) if the U.S. Department of Energy (DOE) data, are:

Electric Power Monthly May 2007 Edition

Electric Power Monthly with data for February 2007
Report Released: May 11ᵗʰ, 2007

Next Release Date: Mid-June 2007

Table 2.1.A. Coal: Consumption for Electricity Generation by Sector, 1993 through February 2007 (Thousand Tons)

Period	Total (All Sectors)	Electric Power Sector		Commercial Sector	Industrial Sector
		Electric Utilities	Independent Power Producers		
2007					
January	92,101	68,616	22,820	78	586
February	83,972	62,454	20,902	80	537
Total	176,073	131,070	43,722	158	1,123

Coal consumption for electric power generation by Electric Utilities in January 2007 = 68,616,000 tons

Electric Utilities used 68,616/92,101 = 0.7450 of coal used for electricity generation in January 2007.

Table 4.2. Receipts, Average Cost and Quality of Fossil Fuels: Electric Utilities, 1993 through January 2007

Period	Coal[1]					Petroleum Liquids[2]				
	Receipts		Average Cost		Avg. Sulfur %	Receipts		Average Cost		Avg. Sulfur %
	(billion Btu)	(1000 tons)	(dollars/ 10⁶ Btu)	(dollars/ton)		(billion Btu)	(1000 barrels)	(dollars/10⁶ Btu)	(dollars/ barrel)	
2007										
January	1,341,204	66,343	1.76	35.63	0.9	15,186	2,410	7.54	47.49	0.7

Cost of coal $ 35.63 ton. (Apparently there was a slight draw down of inventory since 66,343,000 tons were received but 68,616,000 tons used).

Total cost of coal used for electricity generation by Electric Utilities in January, 2007

= $35.63 x 66.343 million

= $2.364 billion

Table 5.1. Retail Sales of Electricity to Ultimate Customers: Total by End-Use Sector, 1993 through February 2007 (Million Kilowatthours)

Period	Residential	Commercial[1]	Industrial[1]	Transportation[1]	Other	All Sectors
2007						
January	125,304	107,427	81,067		704	-- 314,501

Table 5.3. Average Retail Price of Electricity to Ultimate Customers: Total by End-Use Sector, 1993 through February 2007 (Cents per Kilowatthour)

Period	Residential	Commercial[1]	Industrial[1]	Transportation[1]	Other	All Sectors
2007						
January	10.05	9.11	6.12	9.5	--	8.72

Gross (retail) revenue from all electricity sales:

$314,501 x 0.0872 million = $27.424 billion.

Figure 1: Net Generation Shares by Energy Source:
Total (All Sectors), Year-to-Date through February, 2007

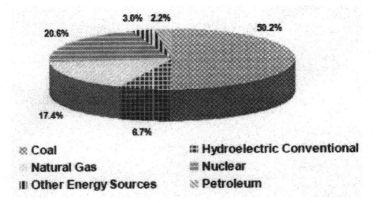

Gross (retail) revenue from all coal-based electricity sales:

$27.424 x 0.502 billion = $13.77 billion

Gross (retail) revenue from coal-based electricity from electric utilities (based on proportion of total coal used):

$ 13.77 x 0.7450 billion = $ 10.256 billion

Coal represents:

(100 x 2.364)/10.256 =   23.05% cost of retail electricity for coal-based electric utilities.

Carbon Dioxide Emission Factors for Coal

by

B.D. Hong and E. R. Slatick

(This article was originally published in Energy Information Administration, *Quarterly Coal Report, January-April 1994*, DOE/ EIA-0121(94/Q1) (Washington, DC, August 1994), pp. 1-8.)

The typical carbon content for coal (dry basis) ranges from more than 60 percent for lignite to more than 80 percent for anthracite.

1 pound of carbon combines with 2.667 pounds of oxygen to produce 3.667 pounds of carbon dioxide. For example, coal with a carbon content of 78 percent and a heating value of 14,000 BTU per pound emits about 204.3 pounds of carbon dioxide per million Btu when completely burned.(5) Complete combustion of 1 short ton (2,000 pounds) of this coal will generate about 5,720 pounds (2.86 short tons) of carbon dioxide.

If the coal used averaged 75% carbon then a $ 100 ton tax on *carbon dioxide* would correspond to:

$ 100/3.667 = $ 27.27 ton tax on *carbon*, and a

$ 27.27*0.75 = $20.45 ton tax on *coal*.

From Table 4.2 we have an average cost for coal of $35.63 per ton, so a tax of $20.45 per ton of coal would raise the price of coal to $56.08 per ton, or by 57.40%.

If coal represents 23.05% of the cost of retail electricity, raising its price by 56.08% would raise the price of retail electricity by:

23.05 x 0.5608 = 12.93 percent

Let us suppose we are interested in:

i)   a Bituminous coal with a carbon content of 75%,

ii) halving the demand for coal based electricity,

iii) coal currently contributes 23.05% of the cost of electricity,

iv) the elasticity of demand for electricity is 1.0 (i.e. people spend a constant amount on electricity, if price goes up they cut consumption enough to leave their electricity bill unaffected), and

v) the coal currently costs $35.63 a metric ton.

To halve consumption, we have to double the price of electricity (from (iv)).

Before tax, a metric ton of coal costing $35.63, generated electricity retailing for $154.58 (since it represented 23.05% of the cost (v) and (iii)). Capital and other costs thus represent $ 118.95 = 154.58 – 35.63

After tax we want the same electricity to retail for $309.16, say $310.00, in order to halve demand. That is we need to raise the price of coal from $35.63 a metric ton to $191.05, that is we want a tax of $155.42 a metric ton. (Other costs are $118.95, before tax $35.63 + $118.95 = $154.58, with tax $118.95 + 35.63 + 155.42 = $310.00).

Since this coal contains only 75% carbon, the corresponding carbon tax is:

191.05/0.75 = $254.73 per ton of carbon.

Say a tax of $250.00 per ton of carbon, or
$187.50 per ton of coal =(0.75*250)

<u>Natural Gas</u>: Natural gas is a more consistent fuel approximating 94% methane.

Data:

i) Natural gas has 1055 Joules per British Thermal Unit (BTU):

Table 5.4 Energy Conversions						
	British Thermal Unit	Foot-pounds	Joules	Calories	Kilo-calories	Kilowatt-hours
1 British Thermal Unit	1	777.9	1055	252.0	0.252	2.93×10^{-4}

ii) A "therm" is 100,000 BTUs, and sells at wholesale for about $0.775.

iii) Natural gas has 15.5 metric tons of carbon per terra joule (1,000,000,000,000 joules).

Calculation: A therm has 105,500,000 joules.
A terra joule has = 1,000,000,000,000/105,500,000 therms
= 1,000,000/105.5
= 9,478.67 therms

A therm has = 15.5/9478.67 metric tons of carbon,
= 0.001635 metric tons of carbon.

A carbon tax of $250.00 per ton would work out at
= 250.00*0.001635
= $ 0.41 per therm.

Raising the price of natural gas from $ 0.775 to $1.185 per therm.

<u>Gasoline</u>: A gallon of gasoline produce 20 pounds of carbon dioxide (CO_2) when burned[143]. Carbon has an atomic weight of 12, and CO2 has an atomic weight of 44, hence a gallon of gasoline contains:

(20*12)/44 = 5.45 pounds of carbon

1 gallon of gasoline contains:

5.45/2000 metric tons of carbon.

0.001225 metric tons of carbon.

A $250.00 tax per ton of carbon implies a tax of:

0.001225*250.00 per gallon

$0.31 per gallon.

If levied on crude oil, it should raise the price of crude from $0.80 per gallon of gasoline to $ 1.11 per gallon. It could be argued that since the present cost structure includes $ 0.42 of taxes no further increase is required.

Table 6-1. Retail Regular Gasoline Price Breakdown (Cents Per Gallon) [144]

	2002 Average		March 2003	
	U.S.	**California**	**U.S.**	**California**
Retail Price (including taxes)	134.4	151.4	169.3	210.3
Taxes	*42.0*	*47.6*	*42.0*	*52.0*
Retail Price (excluding taxes)	92.4	103.8	127.3	158.3
Distribution/ Marketing Costs and Profits	*17.0*	*20.7*	*25.5*	*28.0*
Spot Price	75.4	83.1	102.2	130.3
Refining Costs and Profits	*13.1*	*23.9*	*22.4*	*52.6*
Crude Oil Price	62.4	59.2	79.8	77.7

Sources: Retail prices and taxes, EIA; spot prices, Reuters.
Note: Crude oil price is represented by West Texas Intermediate (WTI) for U.S., Alaska North Slope (ANS) for California.

Summary: Impact of a $250.00 tax per m.ton of carbon

Fuel	Unit	Price	Tax	Sum	Tax/Price%
Coal*	m.ton	$ 35	$187	$222	634
Natural Gas	therm	$0.775	$0.41	$1.185	153
Crude Oil	gallon	$0.777	$0	$0	0

* Coal is only 75% carbon, 187 = 250*0.75

These results suggest that coal is a very much cheaper source of carbon than the other two fuels[145], Dessler and Parsons equate a $100 on carbon with a 24 cent tax per gallon of gasoline. This would imply that a $250.00 tax on carbon would result in a $0.60 tax on gasoline. This is in rough agreement with the above calculations ($ 0.60 versus $ 0.73) if we take existing taxes as given.

The above calculations assumed unit elasticity of demand: That consumers kept their expenditure on electricity constant in the face of higher prices by halving consumption when the price doubled. Other assumptions are possible. If demand is "inelastic" consumers try to maintain consumption in the face of price rises, leading to very high taxes needed to halve consumption. However experience in Californian where electricity rates are about 50% higher than the national average, but power consumption is only 7,000 kilowatt-hours per person, as compared to the national average of 13,000 kilowatt hours per person, suggests that electricity demand may well be elastic. In which case a doubling of price (supported by an extension program to help consumers save electricity) could well lead to reductions in use by over 50 percent.

If demand is "elastic" consumers lower their total expenditure on the item when price rises. Since we are interested in consumption of fossil-based electricity, *people could maintain their expenditure on electricity while reducing expenditures on fossil-based electricity.* They would substitute carbon-free electricity for fossil-electricity. To get a feel for the magnitudes involved suppose that it is only necessary to raise the price of fossil-electricity to halve consumption.

(Since consumers will have no preference *per se* for fossil or fossil-free electricity, we are really talking about *supply response*: how much extra fossil-free electricity would be made available at higher prices.)

Coal: A 50% rise in the price of electricity would take the price from $35.63 to $77.29 per m.ton of coal used. Requiring the price of coal to taxed at the rate of $41.66 a ton, or a tax of 117%. Since coal is 75% carbon this represents a carbon tax of $156.00 a ton, say $150.00 per ton of carbon.

Natural Gas: A carbon tax of $150.00 per ton would work out at

$$= 150.00*0.001635$$

$$= \$ 0.245 \text{ per therm.}$$

Raising the price of natural gas from $ 0.775 to$1.02 per therm.

Gasoline: A $150.00 tax per ton of carbon implies a tax of:

$$0.001225*150.00 \text{ per gallon}$$

$$= \$0.18 \text{ per gallon}$$

Summary: Impact of a $150.00 tax per m.ton of carbon

Fuel	Unit	Price	Tax	Tax/Price%
Coal	m.ton	$ 35	$113	322
Natural Gas	therm	$0.775	$1.02	132
Crude Oil	gallon	$0.777	$0.0	0

Annex 6. What Is In A Barrel of Crude Oil[146]?

Petroleum Products Yielded from One Barrel of Crude Oil in California

Product Percent of Total

Lubricants 0.9%
Other Refined Products 1.5%
Asphalt & Road Oil 1.7%
Liquified Refinery Gas 2.8%
Residual Fuel Oil 3.3%
Marketable Coke 5.0%
Still Gas 5.4%
Jet Fuel 12.3%
Distillate Fuel Oil 15.3%
Gasoline 51.4%

Product	Percent of Total
Finished Motor Gasoline	51.4%
Distillate Fuel Oil	15.3%
Jet Fuel	12.6%
Still Gas	5.4%
Marketable Coke	5.0%
Residual Fuel Oil	3.3%
Liquefied Refinery Gas	2.8%
Asphalt and Road Oil	1.9%
Other Refined Products	1.5%
Lubricants	0.9%

One barrel contains 42 gallons of crude oil. The total volume of products made from crude oil based origins is 48.43 gallons on average - 6.43 gallons greater than the original 42 gallons of crude oil. This represents a "processing gain" due to the additional other petroleum products such as alkylates are added to the refining process to create the final products.

Additionally, California gasoline contains approximately 5.7 percent by volume of ethanol, a non-petroleum-based additive that brings the total processing gain to 7.59 gallons (or 49.59 total gallons).

Source: California Energy Commission, Fuels Office, PIIRA database. Based on 2004 data.

Annex 7: The Luntz Companies on Climate

(Extract from The Luntz Research Companies—Straight Talk pages 131 to 146) http://www.luntzspeak.com/graphics/LuntzResearch. Memo.pdf

THE ENVIRONMENT:
A CLEANER, SAFER, HEALTHIER AMERICA

The core of the Democrat argument depends on the belief that "***Washington Regulations***" represent the best way to preserve the environment. We don't agree.

1) ***First, assure your audience that you are committed to "preserving and protecting the environment, but that "it can be done more wisely and effectively".*** (Absolutely do not raise economic arguments first.) Tell them a personal story from your life. Since many Americans believe Republicans do not care about the environment, ***you will never convince people to accept your ideas until you confront this suspicion and put it to rest.***

2) ***Provide specific examples of federal bureaucrats failing to meet their responsibilities to protect the environment.*** Do not attack the ***principles*** behind existing legislation. Focus instead on the way it is enforced or carried out, and use rhetorical questions.

3) ***Your plan must be put in terms of the future , not the past or present.*** We are carrying forward a legacy, yes, but we are trying to make things even better for the future. ***The environment is an area where people expect progress***, and when they do not see progress being made, they get frustrated.

4) **The three words Americans are looking for in an environmental policy, they are "safer", "cleaner" and "healthier".** Two words that summarize what Americans

are expecting from regulators are "accountability" and "responsibility".

5) ***Stay away from "risk assessment", "cost benefit analysis", and other traditional environmental terminology used by industry and corporations***. Your constituents don't know what these terms mean, and they will then assume that you are pro-business.

6) ***If you must use the economic argument, stress that you are seeking "a fair balance" between the environment and the economy.*** Be prepared to specify and quantify the jobs lost because of needless, excessive or redundant regulations.

7) ***Describe the limited role for Washington.*** We must ***thoroughly review*** the environmental regulations already in place, decide which ones we still need, identify those which no longer make sense, and make sure we don't add any unnecessary rules. Washington should disclose the expected cost of current and new environmental regulations. ***The public has a right to know.***

8) ***Emphasize common sense.*** In making regulatory decisions, we should use best estimates and realistic assumptions, not the worst-case scenarios advanced by environmentalists.

<u>WINNING THE CLOBAL WARMING DEBATE</u>
<u>– AN OVERVIEW</u>
(page 137)

Please keep in mind the following communication recommendations as you address global warming in general, particularly as Democrats and opinion leaders attack President Bush over Kyoto.

1. ***The scientific debate remains open***. Voters believe that there is ***no consensus*** about global warming within the scientific community. Should the public come to believe that the scientific issues are settled, their views about global

warming will change accordingly. Therefore , *you need to continue to make the lack of scientific certainty a primary issue in the debate*, and defer to scientists and other experts in the field.

2. *Americans want a free and open discussion*. Even though Democrats savaged President Bush for formally withdrawing from the Kyoto accord, the truth is that none of them would have actually voted to ratify the treaty, and they were all glad to see it die. Emphasize the importance of *"acting only with all the facts in hand"* and *"making the right decision, not the quick decision."*

3. *Technology and innovation are the key arguments on both sides.* Global warming alarmists use American superiority in technology and innovation quite effectively in responding to accusations that international agreements such as the Kyoto accord could cost the Untied States billions. Rather than condemning corporate America the way most environmentalists have done in the past, they attack their us (sic) for lacking faith in our collective ability to meet any economic challenge presented by environmental changes we make. This should be our argument. *We* need to emphasize how *voluntary* innovation and experimentation are preferable to bureaucratic or international intervention and regulation.

4. *The "international fairness" issue is the home run*. Given the chance, Americans will demand that all nations be part of any international global warming treaty. Nations such as China, Mexico and India would have to sign such an agreement for the majority of Americans to support it.

5. *The economic argument should be secondary*. Many of you will want to focus on the higher prices and lost jobs that would result form complying with Kyoto, but you can do better. Yes, when put in specific terms (food and fuel prices, for example) on an individual-by-individual basis, the argument does resonate. Yes, the fact that Kyoto would hurt the economic well being of seniors and the poor is of

particular concern. However, the economic argument is less effective than each of the arguments listed above.

…. Page 138

The most important principle in any discussion of global warming is your commitment to sound science. Americans unanimously believe all environmental rules and regulations should be based on sound science and common sense. Similarly, our confidence in the ability of science and technology to solve our nation's ills is second to none. Both perceptions will work in your favor if properly cultivated.

The scientific debate is closing [against us] but is not yet closed. There is still a window of opportunity to challenge the science. Americans believe that all strange weather that was associated with El Nino had something to do with global warming, and there is little you can do to convince them otherwise. However, a handful of people believes the science of global warming is a close question. Most Americans want more information so that they can make an informed decision. It is our job to provide that information.

Language that Works: *"We must not rush to judgment before all the facts are in. We need to ask more questions. We deserve more answers. And until we learn more, we should not commit America to any international document that handcuffs us either now or in the future"*.

Words that Work: *"Scientists can extrapolate all kinds of things from today's data, but that doesn't tell us anything about tomorrow's world. You can't look back a million years and say that proves that we're heating the globe now hotter than it has been. After all, just 20 years ago scientist were worried about a new ice age."*

Wilfred Candler

CONCLUSION: REDEFINING LABELS
(page 143)

The mainstream, centrist American now sees the excesses of so-called "environmentalists" and prefer the label "conservationist" instead. These individuals are still clearly "pro-environment" but not at the expense of everything else in life. They are the kind of voter who considers the environment as one of a variety of factors in their decision for whom to vote, but not the overriding factor. If we win these people over, we win the debate: It's that simple. The rest is commentary.

......

WE have spent the last seven years examining how best to communicate complicated ideas and controversial subjects. The terminology in the upcoming environmental debate needs refinement, starting with "global warming" and ending with "environmentalism". *It's time for us to start talking about "climate change" instead of global warming and "conservation" instead of preservation.*

1. *"Climate change" is less frightening than "global warming".* As one focus group participant noted, climate change "sounds like you're going from Pittsburgh to Fort Lauderdale". While global warming has catastrophic connotations attached to it, climate change suggests a more controllable and less emotional challenge.

2. *We should be "conservationists", not "preservationists" or "environmentalists".* The term "conservationist" has far more positive connotations than either of the other terms. It conveys a moderate, reasoned, common sense position between replenishing the earth's natural resources and the human need to make use of those resources.

202

Annex 8: More on Modeling

There are three bases for believing that global warming is real. The first is historical data obtained from ice-cores for times long past (up to 800,000 years ago) and from atmospheric sampling of CO2 in the last 50 years. The second is everyday observation, and the third is from climate and economic "models".

These models are not physical constructs, but rather are sets of equations that trace out how variables interact with each other over time. Conceptually simple, models have become large and opaque. Climate models are large because they want to achieve global coverage, over decades, for phenomena that interact at close range and over a short time interval. Both are opaque because they are written in a meta-language that is intelligible to the computer and the researched. Consider the equation:

$$TotalEmissions = CoalEmissions + GasEmissions$$
$$+ OilEmissions + CementEmissions.$$

Where in lower-level languages the "=" sign would direct the computer to "replace the variable on the left by the expression on the right". In such lower level languages "C", "Fortran", "Delphi", etc, only one variable can appear on the left.

In higher-level meta languages GAMS and GEMPACK, the expression means "find the unknown variable in the expression and calculate its value on the basis of the known variables". Thus in these higher level languages the above expression can also be represented:

$$CoalEmissions + GasEmissions + OilEmissions$$
$$+ CementEmissions = TotalEmissions,$$

Or even

$$TotalEmissions - CoalEmissions =$$
$$GasEmissions + OilEmissions +$$
$$CementEmissions.$$

Which is of course confusing since you do not know *a priori* which variable is the unknown in the equation.

To further confuse (or simplify, depending on your point of view) matters, typically the researcher will shorten the variable names, such as:

VARIABLE TE

> ! TE = TotalEmissions !

> set source (CE , GE, OE, ME)

> ! CE = CoalEmissions !

> ! GE = GasEmissions !

> ! OE = OilEmissions !

> ! ME = CementEmissions !

where the "comment" within the exclamation marks is intended to be helpful to researchers, and is not read by the computer.

We are now ready to write the basic equation in machine and (possibly) human readable form:

formula TE = **sum**(all,i,source(i))

Where "**formula**" warns the computer that this is a relationship that is to be "solve" or satisfied,
TE is, of course TotalEmissions
sum is an instruction to the computer to add what follows,
all, i, instructs the computer to sum over all i indexes in the following expression,
source(i) identifies the set to which the i index is to be applied.

This rather protracted discussion is to explain why models that may be conceptually simple are nevertheless inaccessible to the ordinary reader.

When in the 60's large scale models were first being developed there were no meta languages, so that a researcher would write a program in Fortran, C or other lower language, and then write a separate article explaining what his model was *intended* to do, and the results obtained. "Intended" here is crucial, since from time to time it was found that the actual Fortan instructions did not faithfully represent what the researcher had intended. (Instead of "Revenue = price*quantity", (revenue = price times quantity) the researchers actual computer program might have had "Revenue = price/quantity" (revenue = price divided by quantity) quite a different relationship).

With the higher level languages, we know exactly what the computer was told to do (that is, if we can follow the instructions!), and can thus check on the veracity of the researchers report. However, the capacity to do this check now depends on learning a meta language. And try reading even the above model without the optional comments! Researchers are free to use any mnemonics intelligible to them. Frequently the mnemonics chosen have no intuitive interpretation to the uninitiated (as for example ME above).

Not only is there the challenge of learning a meta language, but once learnt, the model itself may include hundreds of lines of code. Large models often have been developed over time by a series of Ph.D. students who have added and refined individual sections of the model. Thus trying to fully understand a model is not something that should be undertaken lightly.

How can we come to trust model results if we do not know exactly what is going on inside the "black box"? By asking about data inputs and outputs, and comparing these with actual empirical data; and by being quite clear as to the overall logic of the model: *To at least understand what is being modeling, even if the specifics of how this is done eludes us.*

As described in the text there are currently three distinct types of global warming models:

i) IPCC carbon-cycle models, and

ii) GTAP based economic growth/pollution models.

iii) DICE and RICE "quick and simple" integrated models.

GTAP stands for Global Trade Analysis Project, which is headquartered in the Department of Agricultural Economics, at Purdue University.

IPCC carbon-cycle models: There are about a dozen IPCC carbon-cycle models, distinguished by how they divide the oceans and atmosphere into distinct boxes, and how ambitious they are in dealing with various aspect of climate change, such as cloud cover, terrestrial glacial mechanics, non-CO2 greenhouse gasses, forest fires, permafrost melting, natural heating, ocean carbon sequestration and the like. They all have the same basic mechanism: Initialized with data from a given date, and driven by exogenous (pre-determined) levels of AFCO2TA, they apply physical laws to see how climate ACO2 and temperature would evolve. Any one model can, of course, be run with a whole range of alternative scenarios for the time-sequence of AFCO2TA, and the same time sequence can be used on different models and the results compared. IPCC carbon-cycle models are the ones that give predictions as to changes in the concentration of ACO2, temperature changes, ice-melting, sea-level rise, drought, fire and flood in 50 to 100 years. As shown in Figure 4, the models give a good fit to observed temperature for the last 100 year or so. Note, however that this fit is the result of being given actual AFCO2TA on a year by year basis.

Different forecast patterns of AFCO2TA in future years will lead to different projections with respect to temperature and other aspects of global warming. Any particular time profile of AFCO2TA is described as a "scenario". In discussion of model results there is frequent reference to changes from business as usual (BAU). The initial climate modeling undertaken for the Montreal protocol on fluorocarbons had an explicit BAU scenario for fluorocarbon use. However, although in discussion of global warming there is frequent reference to the concept of BAU the IPCC has not defined any such scenario[147]. This may reflect the political nature of the IPCC process, with countries (such as the U.S. and Australia) committed to minimal interference with BAU, not wishing to have the results of their policies described in graphic detail, or (less conspiratorially) the IPCC scientists may have concluded that strict BAU was no longer a plausible scenario after the Kyoto agreement came into force.

However a wide range of non-BAU possibilities have been modeled. Four basic scenarios/storylines have been defined:

"The storylines describe developments in many different social, economic, technological, environmental, and policy dimensions. The titles of the storylines have been kept simple: A1, A2, B1 and B2. There is no particular order among the storylines; they are listed in the alphabetic and numeric order:

- The A1 storyline and scenario family describes a future world of very rapid economic growth, low population growth, and the rapid introduction of new and more efficient technologies. Major underlying themes are convergence among regions, capacity building and increased cultural and social interactions, with a substantial reduction in regional differences in per capita income. The A1 scenario family develops into four groups that describe alternative directions of technological change in the energy system [8]

- The A2 storyline and scenario family describes a very heterogeneous world. The underlying theme is self-reliance and preservation of local identities. Fertility patterns across regions converge very slowly, which results in high population growth. Economic development is primarily regionally oriented and per capita economic growth and technological change are more fragmented and slower than in other storylines.

- The B1 storyline and scenario family describes a convergent world with the same low population growth as in the A1 storyline, but with rapid changes in economic structures toward a service and information economy, with reductions in material intensity, and the introduction of clean and resource-efficient technologies. The emphasis is on global solutions to economic, social, and environmental sustainability, including improved equity, but without additional climate initiatives.

- The B2 storyline and scenario family describes a world in which the emphasis is on local solutions to economic, social, and environmental sustainability. It is a world with moderate population growth, intermediate levels of economic development, and less rapid and more diverse technological change than in the B1 and A1 storylines. While the scenario is also oriented toward environmental protection and social equity, it focuses on local and regional levels.[148]"

In turn six modeling groups in four countries (Japan, America, Netherlands and Austria) have developed models (with different technical specifications and degrees of disaggregation) that have run these model to obtain global (and some regional) results. In all there are 40 distinct scenarios have been run under the auspices of the IPCC program. (as remarked above, none of which attempts to model BAU).

Table 8.1: Emission Levels for A1 (Rapid Growth) and ASF (Atmospheric Stabilization Framework)[149]

IPCC SRES Emissions Scenarios - Version 1.1

World - A1 ASF		1990	2000	2010	2020	2030	2040	2050
Population	Million	5264	6117	6827	7537	8039	8526	8704
GNP/GDP (mex) Trillion US$		20.9	28.9	41.3	60.7	87.9	146.0	174.3
Cumulative CO2 Emissions	GtC	0.0	75.3	170.8	306.0	488.7	709.7	960.5
Carbon Sequestraction	GtC	-1.8	-1.8	-1.7	-1.7	-1.7	-1.7	-1.6
Anthropogenic Emissions (standardized)								
Fossil Fuel CO2	GtC	5.99	6.90	10.01	14.67	19.49	22.60	25.72
Other CO2	GtC	1.11	1.07	1.12	1.24	1.13	0.98	0.84
Total CO2	GtC	7.10	7.97	11.13	15.91	20.62	23.59	26.56

IPCC SRES Emissions Scenarios - Version 1.1

World - A1 ASF		2060	2070	2080	2090	2100
Population	Million	8527	8444	8022	7282	7056
GNP/GDP (mex) Trillion US$		225.7	257.3	367.8	484.9	531.9
Cumulative CO2 Emissions	GtC	1216.8	1454.8	1674.9	1878.2	2065.5
Carbon Sequestraction	GtC	-1.6	-1.5	-1.5	-1.4	-1.4
Anthropogenic Emissions (standardized)						
Fossil Fuel CO2	GtC	24.14	22.55	20.97	19.37	17.78
Other CO2	GtC	0.84	0.58	0.32	0.18	0.16
Total CO2	GtC	26.56	24.72	22.87	21.15	19.53

Table 8.1 gives the CO2 related data used to define one scenario. It is not entirely clear how to read these tables, since "standardized", the way cumulative emission are calculated, and the computation of successive decadal emissions are not defined.

Table 8.2 Actual Carbon Usage 1986 to 2003. (MtC)[150]

Year	Total	%	Gas	Liquids	Solids	Prod-uction	Flaring	Cap-ital
......								
1986	5600	830	2297	2290	137	46	1.13	
1987	5731	2.3	893	2309	2341	143	44	1.14
1988	5958	4.0	935	2416	2405	152	50	1.16
1989	6072	1.9	972	2464	2440	156	40	1.17
1990	6143	1.2	1025	2542	2378	157	40	1.16
1991	6252	1.8	1085	2653	2308	161	44	1.16
1992	6121	-2.1	1099	2534	2285	167	36	1.12
1993	6129	0.1	1118	2573	2225	176	37	1.11
1994	6262	2.2	1133	2608	2298	186	37	1.11
1995	6402	2.2	1152	2643	2375	196	36	1.13
1996	6560	2.5	1211	2694	2416	203	36	1.14
1997	6696	4.6	1208	2816	2425	209	37	1.14
1998	6656	-0.6	1245	2860	2311	209	31	1.14
1999	6522	-2.0	1276	2806	2191	217	31	1.11
2000	6672	2.6	1318	2914	2183	226	31	1.10
2001	6842	2.5	1341	2903	2338	236	24	1.11
2002	6973	1.9	1371	2877	2450	252	24	1.12
2003	7303	4.7	1402	2981	2624	275	21	1.14

Only for 1990 and 2000 is there comparable data in Giga tons of carbon as shown in Table 8.3.

Table 8.3 Comparison of Scenario and Actual
CO2 Emissions (GtC)

-----------ASF------------   Oak Ridge National Laboratory

Year	FossilCO2	OtherCO2	TotalCO2	FossilCO2	%
1990	5.99	1.11	7.10	6.14	-2.4
2000	6.90	1.07	7.97	6.67	3.4
Change	0.91			0.53	

For the moment the ASF (Atmospheric Stabilization Framework) simulation seems to be reasonably close to actual emissions as reported by Oak Ridge National Laboratory, although the simulated emissions are rising significantly faster than reported. (Oak Ridge included cement production as a source of emission, which may or may not be in the IPCC model). As shown in Tables 8.4 and 8.5, for the ASF model, the four basic scenarios do not begin to diverge until after 2000.

Table 8.4 Comparison of Annual Fossil CO2 Emissions by
Scenario (GtC)

Scenario	1990	2000	2010	2050	2100
A1-ASF	5.99	6.90	10.	25.72	17.78
A2-ASF	5.99	6.90	8.46	16.49	28.91
B1-ASF	5.99	6.90	9.65	17.50	6.27
B2-ASF	5.99	6.90	8.85	15.42	18.93

Table 8.5 Comparison of Cumulative Fossil CO2 Emissions by Scenario (GtC)

Scenario	1990	2000	2010	2050	2100
A1-ASF	0.00	75.3	179.8	960.5	2,065.5
A2-ASF	0.00	75.3	163.1	728.6	1,855.3
B1-ASF	0.00	75.3	169.0	803.6	1,382.6
B2-ASF	0.00	75.3	165.1	726.2	1,592.1

The annual fossil CO2 emissions in Table 8.4 (and resulting cumulative emissions in Table 8.5) are *inputs* to the model, justified by the scenario or storyline. The concentration of CO2 in the atmosphere is a model *output* determined in part by the emissions, but also by sequestration, which in turn will depend on temperature, melting of ice-sheets, any induced releases of sequestered CO2, and the like.

While graphical representations of key model outputs are widely available, *tabulations of output values, such as were used to construct Tables 8.4 and 8.5 do not seem to be readily available.*

A final comment on climate (carbon-cycle) models is to remember that they can be used to establish the estimate the effects at *equilibrium* of having any given level of ACO2, or to trace out the year by year impact of continuing AFCO2TA: They can be used in an *equilibrium* or *dis-equilibrium* (more commonly known as *transient*) mode.

GTAP (Global Trade Analysis Project) economic growth/pollution models: While there are a large number of carbon cycle models that have been developed more-or-less independently by national (and in the case of IIASA (International Institute for Applied Systems Analysis) international) climate modeling groups, for economic/ policy modeling there are many models, but only one dominant modeling "language" or framework. This may be a little hard to grasp at first, but a family of computer models (and associated data bases) using a common coding language, data and basic model structure is maintained by GTAP, physically in the agricultural economics department at Purdue University. GTAP was initiated in 1993, and played a big round in the economic/policy analysis underlying the Uruguay Round of trade negotiations.

The basic GTAP model divides the world into 8 regions, each with appropriate industrial and agricultural sectors, investment, savings, consumption and trade. This provides a basic structure available to modelers to add detail depending on their interest. In the case of global warming, primary interest is in the use of fossil fuels and the rate of AFCO2TA. This requires adding to the model information on the carbon intensity of different sectors, and the elasticity of investment in both fossil and fossil free electricity production.

The rate of AFCO2TA depends on patterns of consumption that determine levels of industrial activity and trade that determine (simultaneously) personal income and GDP. Patterns of personal consumption depend on personal income, prices of commodities, which depend on taxes, trade and production costs. The key policy variables that feed through the model to yield rate of AFCO2TA, are taxes, trade barriers, subsidies and particularly support for investments in fossil free technologies.

Different countries or interest groups may be interested in different aspects of global warming, and hence wish to expand the model in the directions that particularly interest them. Any such expansion has to be properly documented, and any new data series contributed to the model data base. This builds the "intellectual capital" of the GTAP project, and is available to subsequent researchers who may wish to enlarge the model in a similar direction. In particular the US Department of Energy and the U.S. Environmental Protection Agency have funded an extension of the basic GTAP model to emphasize energy use, CO_2 emissions, and emissions from changing land use and cultivation technologies, and national and international carbon trading. The structure has been given its own label at model GTAP-E. GTAP-E is an equilibrium model, allowing comparison of situations in which ACO2 has stabilized. It has been used to show that carbon trading between countries with target rates of AFCO2TA, can have knock on effects adversely affecting energy exporting developing countries and providing benefits to developing countries that import energy[151]

There is also a dis-equilbrium/ transitional version G-Dyn-E.

The GTAP data base also supports a fully integrated <u>Emissions Predictions and Policy Model (EPPA)</u> located at MIT. This model divides the world into 17 countries or county groups, 3 non-energy industries, 3 primary factors of production and 7 existing or future energy sources. This economic/policy module interfaces with a climate model. The whole system steps forward 5-years at a time. It takes about 10 hours to run, on

a modern desktop. Currently economic activity (and economic policies) determine releases of CO_2, that affect the climate. There does not yet appear to be a feed-back whereby temperature affects economic activity (particularly demand for air-conditioning and central heating). Because of the disaggregation of the energy sector, it is possible to trace out the likely impact of a carbon tax, carbon trading, international carbon trading, rate of switch between energy generating technologies, etc.

Finally, mention should be made of the <u>DICE (Dynamic Integrated model of Climate and the Economy)</u> and <u>RICE (Regional dynamic Integrated model of Climate and the Economy)</u>. That are much more aggregated models, indeed DICE aggregates all countries into a global economy. These model have the advantage that they can be run quite quickly, and despite the high degree of aggregation get results not inconsistent with the larger models. They are available in Excel spreadsheet form.

Annex 9: Methane Production from Methane Hydrates

Precision Combustion, Inc. (PCI) is developing its downhole catalytic combustor for the purposes of generating downhole heat for efficient production of methane from its hydrate, with potential for CO_2 sequestration. We are developing this as an enabling technology for the long term goal of increasing U.S. and world energy production and available reserves at low cost while potentially reducing global warming.

"Today, the U.S. Geological Survey estimates that methane hydrate may, in fact, contain more organic carbon than all the world's coal, oil, and non-hydrate natural gas combined. The magnitude of this previously unknown global storehouse of methane is truly staggering and has raised serious inquiry into the possibility of using methane hydrate as a source of energy." [U.S. DOE Methane Hydrate Program].

"Extraction of methane from hydrates could provide an enormous energy and petroleum feedstock resource. Additionally, conventional gas resources appear to be trapped beneath methane hydrate layers in ocean sediments." [U.S. Geological Service

Gas hydrates occur in Arctic and marine subsurface regions. Gas hydrate is a crystalline solid consisting of gas molecules, usually methane, each surrounded by a cage of water molecules. The gas is held in this state by a combination of low temperature and high pressure. If the gas could be effectively, safely and controllably tapped, gas hydrates offer the potential for making major contributions to meeting DOE primary objectives regarding energy needs and energy independence while substantially expanding available world energy reserves. Heating offers a high production option for doing this as the heat released from oxidation of a single methane molecule is enough to liberate over ten methane molecules from their hydrate state. (Emphasis added)

PCI is developing this application under a U.S. Department of Energy Small Business Innovation Research Phase I/II contract. Among the results to date:

- Downhole heat generation can produce methane from dissociation of the hydrate

- Only 12-15% of produced methane is consumed in the process, offering substantial energy savings from avoided heat losses

- This approach avoids heating of the permafrost

- Potential CO2 sequestration for added energy savings

This application offers the potential for an economic technology for substantially increasing world available energy reserves.

The technology also may provide a global warming benefit through CO2 sequestration. CO2 hydrate is thermodynamically more stable than methane hydrate, it will exist at a higher temperature than methane hydrate, and the CO2 hydrate heat of formation (exothermic) is slightly greater than the heat of dissociation (endothermic) for methane hydrate. This means the possibility exists for economic sequestration of CO2 into the methane hydrate bed, advantageously stabilizing the bed, and further reducing required heat from combustion.

http://www.precision-combustion.com/methanehydrate.html

Endnotes

[1] *The Weather Makers*, by Tim Flannery, *Field Notes From A Catastrophe*, by Elizabeth Kolbert, *An Inconvenient Truth*, by Al Gore, *Heat: How to Stop the Planet from Burning*, by George Monbiot, *Hell and High Water* by Joseph Romm, *Boiling Point* by Ross Gelspan, and *The Rough Guide to Climate Change* by Robert Henson, and references cited therein, p.329-332. These are all excellent books. Key web-sites are www.carbontax.org and www.heatisonline. org.

[2] *Drought Is Sapping the Southeast, and Its Farmers*, NYTimes, 07/04/07. "Most of the region, government scientists say, is suffering from a rare sharp dry spell, though they are reluctant to attribute it to climate change". No one event can easily be attributed to climate change, but it would be a rare scientist who (without a side payment from the carbon lobby) would assert that it was *not* connected to global warming. The drought is interesting in that it is happening here, in the United States/developed world, when most global warming projections suggest "reassuringly" that it is the developing world that will bear the brunt of global warming. Meanwhile England is having unprecedentedly intense rainfall and associated flooding.

[3] President Bush has proposed the objective of "reducing the energy intensity of the economy", or ACO2 releases per unit of GDP (Gross Domestic Product). All this requires is that the increase in ACO2 releases (not AFCO2TA) be less than the growth in GDP. As ACO2 increased so would global temperatures. Truly: "A village in Texas is missing its idiot".

[4] *The Greening of Planet Earth*, a propaganda video cited in *The Weather Makers*, p240.

[5] Including *The National Wildlife Federation, The Natural Resource Defense Fund, The Nature Conservancy, The Pew Centre on Global Climate Change* and *World Resources Institute*.

[6] Bloomberg News, June20, 2007.

[7] *Pollution Charges for Environmental Protection: A Policy Link Between Energy and the Environment*, R. Stavins and B. Whitehead, Annual Review of Energy and the Environment, 17: 187-210, 1992.

[8] *Probabilistic Integrated Assessment of "Dangerous" Climate Change*, Michael D. Mastrandrea, and S. Schneider. Science 304, 571 (2004).

[9] Eventually, this increased CO2 will tend towards global warming, but volcanoes also emit huge amounts of dust into the higher atmosphere thus shielding the earth from sunlight, and providing an initial cooling influence. Nothing is simple, if we go into the details.

[10] The alkalinity (pH) of the ocean, affects how quickly marine shell animals (and coral) can form their shells, which are eventually deposited to form rock, thus reducing the carbon in the active carbon cycle. By absorbing CO_2 when it is plentiful and releasing it if it is scarce, the oceans serve as a powerful, if slow, buffer on changes in ACO_2: It provides a benign feed-back loop.

[11] *The Rough Guide to Climate Change* , Robert Henson, p.33

[12] As discussed below, Tim Flannery references the Permo-Triassic extinction, when temperatures are thought to have risen by six degrees Centigrade, or more.

[13] Karl Davies, Northampton, MA: 2000; http://www.daviesand.com/Choices/ Precautionary_Planning/New_Data/; used by permission of the Estate of Karl Davies, and http://www.ccs.neu.edu/home/gene/peakoil/co2-400k-years.gif

[14]<a href='http://zfacts.com'> http://zfacts.com/p/194.html </a>

[15] *Compendium of Data on Global Change*, A. Marland, Oak Ridge National Laboratory, 2006, Quoted in *Dangerous Human-Made Interference with Climate*, Dr James Hansen, Testimony to Select Committee on Energy Independence and Global Warming, U.S. House of Representative, 26 April 2007.

[16] Bloomberg News, June20, 2007.

[17] http://celebrating200years.noaa.gov/datasets/mauna/image3b.html

[18] *Heat: How to stop the planet from burning*, George Monbiot. P.10.

[19] Ibid, p 10.

[20] Ibid, p. 11.

[21] *Hell and High Water and what we should do*, Joseph Romm, p.68

[22] The Weather Makers, p. 200.

[23] These are not by any means simple calculations, since a change in ACO_2 affects the rate at which the ocean will absorb CO_2,

[24] "The Weather Makers", Chapter 4.

[25]   http://www.pbs.org/newshour/bb/environment/jan-june06/globalwarming_ 06-08.html

[26] http://magma.nationalgeographic.com/ngm/0402/feature5/online_extra.html

[27] http://www.eia.doe.gov/oiaf/1605/ggccebro/chapter1.html

[28] Bloomberg News, June 20, 2007.

[29] NYTimes, p C5, July 6th, 2007.

[30] http://www.npr.org/templates/story/story.php?storyId=5356683.

[31] Evidence of a high elasticity of demand (strong reduction in demand in the face of a price rise) is presented in Chapter 3.

[32] Sometimes referred to as "the tragedy of the commons" (more accurately the problem of "open access resources") and the insight that "what belongs to everyone, belongs to no one": Individually we will not look after a resource that will benefit someone else, or as Larry Summers famously remarked "no one ever washed a rental car".

[33] There are suggestions that the genocide in Darfur, can be traced to twin problems of declining rainfall and rapidly rising population, leading to rapidly falling food production per capita (together with loss of traditional grazing lands due to declining rainfall). When the full story is analyzed, we may yet find that Darfur is better described as the first (perhaps of many) ecocides. (*Darfur: Relief in a vulnerable environment*, Tearfund, www.tearfund.org, 2007.)

[34] As I write these words, I know that my computer and table light are almost certainly AFCO2TA (adding fossil carbon dioxide to the atmosphere). I hear no muffled screams, but perhaps I should.

[35] *The Economics of Climate Change: The Stern Review*, Nicholas Stern, pp 276.

[36] http://www.eia.doe.gov/oiaf/1605/ggrpt/pdf/executive_summary.pdf

[37] *The Economics of Climate Change: The Stern Review*, Nicholas Stern, p. 16.

[38] Ibid, p.12. Or 380 mpp of CO2 = 32 implies 380/0.88 = 432 ppm of CO2e.

[39] http://www.esrl.noaa.gov/gmd/ccgg/trends/

[40] *A comparative analysis of woody biomass and coal for electricity generation under various CO2 emission reductions and taxes,* J. Gan and C.T. Smith, Biomass and Bioenergy, 30 (2006), pp. 296-303.

[41] The latest IPCC report highlights need for integrated climate/human behavior models:

"Adapting to the global climate change impacts outlined in the IPCC's Working Group 2 Report, 'Climate Change 2007: Impacts, Adaptation and Vulnerability', will require new evaluation tools to help choose the best way forward, according to the International Geosphere-Biosphere Programme (IGBP), an international network of environmental scientists.

This quest for adaptation strategies opens a new chapter in global environmental change research that requires not only continued development of sophisticated climate models (and understanding the processes behind them) but also a new integration of those models with predictive descriptions of human behavior."

http://www.eurekalert.org/pub_releases/2007-04/igp-lir040607.php.

[42] Income elasticity (how we change consumption patterns as we get richer), price elasticity (how we reduce consumption when prices rise) and innovation elasticity (how we change our innovation effort as prices change).

[43] http://www.princeton.edu/pr/news/04/q3/0812-carbon/backgrounder.pdf

[44] But avoiding corn-ethanol that requires 74 units of fossil energy to produce 100 units of ethanol energy. If ethanol was used to produce the ethanol, four liters of corn-ethanol would need to be produced to have one to sell to motorists. *The Rough Guide to Climate Change*, p. 307.

[45] http://www.washingtonpost.com/wp-dyn/content/article/2007/03/05/AR2007030501493.html and http://www.washingtonpost.com/wp-dyn/content/graphic/2007/03/06/GR2007030600396.html?referrer=emaillink and "Fighting Global Warming One House at a Time" a DVD available from Chesapeake Climate Action Network. (chesapeakeclimate.org).

[46] Heat: How to Stop the Planet from Burning, George Monbiot, pp. 68-71, and http://www.passiv.de/

[47] The 2030 Challenge has been adopted and supported by the US Conference of Mayors, American Institute of Architects, US Green Building Council, International Council for Local Environmental Initiatives, National Association of Counties and numerous states, counties and cities. For more information see www.architecture2030.org.

[48] Economists will note that a 50% higher electricity price (supported by an active support program from the utilities) has resulted in consumption levels almost half the national average. Benign climate may help, but the suggestion is that electricity demand is elastic. Unit elasticity would have required a doubling in price to halve use.

[49] Hell and High Water, and what we should do, Joseph Romm, pp 163-173.

[50] Executive on a Mission: Save the Planet, NYTimes, 5/22/2007.

[51] A more complete discussion of this topic is available at: http://www.carbontradewatch.org/pubs/carbon_neutral_myth.pdf

[52] http://www.ecobusinesslinks.com/carbon_offset_wind_credits_carbon_reduction.htm
Note underlines "_" between words.

[53] This is not a fantasy, but a carbon credit scheme actually on offer by carbonfund.org in 2007.

[54] http://www.carbontradewatch.org/pubs/carbon_neutral_myth.pdf

[55] NYTimes, 1/1/2007, page C4.

[56] Just as the Medieval sinner, indulgence in hand, had nevertheless sinned.

[57] On reading the fine print even of what is claimed, this low price depends on waiting a century for the AFCO2TA to be removed from atmosphere (Annex 3). At which stage the sequestration ceases as light bulbs wear out, and trees die.

[58] http://en.wikipedia.org/wiki/Clean_coal

[59] The Future of Coal--Options for a Carbon Constrained World, MIT, 2007

[60] Given the way carbon credits are generated (Chapter 4) it would not be surprising to find utilities selling carbon credit because they could have built less efficient plants than they did!

[61] Methane Extraction and Carbon Sequestration, ORNL (Oak Ridge National Laboratory) Review Vol35, No. 2, 2002.

[62] i.e. Government would bear half the risk that the site proved unsatisfactory.

[63] "Liquefied Coal Gains Support as Fuel of the Future", NYTimes, 5/29/2007, page C8.

[64] NYTimes 5/29/2007.

[65] http://money.cnn.com/2007/05/24/news/economy/bc.usa.coal.fuels.reut/index.htm

[66] But Obama only supports coal-derived fuels that emit less carbon than gasoline, http://money.cnn.com/2007/05/24/news/economy/bc.usa.coal.fuels.reut/index.htm

So what is he doing co-sponsoring a Coal-to-Liquid Support Bill, that does not include his caveat? With current technologies coal-derived fuels emit more carbon than gasoline. It is as simple as that.

[67] Methane Extraction and Carbon Sequestration, ORNL (Oak Ridge National Laboratory) Review Vol35, No. 2, 2002.

[68] http://unfccc.int/kyoto_protocol/mechanisms/emissions_trading/items/2731.php,

http://www.science.org.au/nova/054/054key.htm

[69] http://en.wikipedia.org/wiki/Clean_Development_Mechanism, http://www.climnet.org/euenergy/CDM.htm

[70] Since CO2 and methane are both part of the carbon cycle they could be controlled jointly through a cap on the use of fossil carbon.

[71] In early 2007 an issue that had by then already been known for a while erupted in major media. A study published in Nature found that the main type of CDM projects paid as much as 50 times more for the emission reductions than the costs alone would warrant, with the excessive profits ending up with the factories

and the carbon traders. The particular kind of CDM (Clean Development Mechanism) projects in question regard refrigerant-producing factories in non-Annex-1 countries (particularly China) that generate the powerful greenhouse gas HFC 23 as a by-product. By destroying the HFCs, the factories can earn CER (Certified Emission Reduction) credits. Destroying the HFCs requires a simple and relatively cheap piece of equipment called a scrubbers; the author argues it would cost only €100 million to pay producers to capture and destroy HFC 23 compared with €4.6 billion in CDM credits. While this is still cheaper than the typical cost of reducing emissions in industrialized countries, it is seen as a major loophole in the carbon trading system and undermines the tenet of emission trading being as a cost-effective tool for reducing emissions. Also, "HFC 23 emitters can earn almost twice as much from the CDM credits as they can from selling refrigerant gases – by any measure a major distortion of the market," writes the author. In response, Halldor Thorgeirsson, director of sustainable development mechanisms at the UNFCCC claims: "The idea of easy money is out of proportion." And he says the loophole is now closed and that new HFC 23 facilities will no longer be eligible for CDM credits.

http://en.wikipedia.org/wiki/Clean_Development_Mechanism#_ref-5.

The key problem was that HFC23 has 9100 times the heating effect of CO2, over a 20 year period , allowing one ton of HFC reduction to count for 9100 tons of CO2.

[72] Once energy ceases to be "essentially free" a number of sophisticated questions arise as to the physical capacity of the grid, and to what extent inter-temporal trading of carbon credits should be encouraged. Many of these questions are addressed in "Heat: How to stop global warming", by George Monbiot. They are discussed below in Chapter 9, Technology.

[73] In some cases, especially for regulated industries, pricing may be related to a margin over cost, leading to a lower price rise (and lower incentive to economize on electricity).

[74] Alcoa, Alcan, AIG (insurance), BP America, Boston Scientific, Caterpillar, Connoco Phillips, Deere, Dow, Duke Energy, DuPont, Florida Power & Light, General Electric, General Motors, Johnson and Johnson, Lehman Brothers, Marsh, Pacific Gas & Electric, Pepsico, and PNM Resources, Shell and Siemens, have joined Environmental Defense, the Pew Center on Global Climate Change, Natural Resources Defense Council and the World Resources Institute to form an unprecedented alliance — the United States Climate Action Partnership (USCAP). http://www.environmentaldefense.org/article.cfm?contentID=5828, posted 22nd January 2007. BP, Duke Energy, DuPont, and General Motors, were formerly members of the Climate Change Coalition.

[75] Fred Krupp, President of Environmental Defense Fund (salary $ 415,000) was the subject of a profile article in the New Republic, 9/24/2007. He is described as the "master of the deal" bringing environmental advocates and polluters around

the table to achieve an agreement that advances both agendas. This has worked well in establishing a market for pollution credits in sulfur emissions. However, the problem with global warming is that we need to phase out completely the use of fossil fuels. This means that the interests of the citizenry and energy companies are in direct opposition. A deal satisfactory to one is ipso facto unlikely to be satisfactory to the other. A C&T scheme where all caps dropped to zero over a decade would be a serious contender for "best policy", however neither EDF nor its corporate partners are advocating such a drastic, and necessary, C&F scheme.

[76] http://news.bbc.co.uk/1/hi/uk_politics/6167671.stm

[77] A florescent bulb may use a quarter of the electricity used by an incandescent bulb, but there is no guarantee that this smaller amount of electricity will not be provided from a fossil-power-plant.

[78] Say there was a 20% tax on fossil based electricity. The price of all electricity to consumers would likely rise by 20%, however competition amongst electricity suppliers for fossil-free electricity would drive up the price of fossil-free electricity from the suppliers, be they wind farms, nuclear or hydro. Thus an incentive would be provided to invest in fossil-free electricity generation.

[79] http://cdiac.ornl.gov/trends/emis/top2003.tot "Ranking of the world's countries by 2003 total CO2 emissions from fossil-fuel burning, cement production, and gas flaring. Emissions (CO2_TOT) are expressed in thousand metric tons of carbon (not CO2)." 1 ton of cement emits 0.5 tons of CO2 (not carbon) from calcining limestone. http://www.buildinggreen.com/features/flyash/appendixa.cfm.

[80] The $250 carbon tax is based on the assumption of unit elasticity of demand for electricity: If price is doubled, consumption is halved. In fact, as observed in Annex 5, and Chapter 3, Californian electricity rates are about 50% higher than the national average, while power consumption is only 7,000 kilowatt-hours per person, as compared to the national average of 13,000 kilowatt hours per person. While there may be non-price reasons for per capita electricity consumption to be lower in California, this still suggests that demand for electricity is elastic. And given a reasonable supply response from fossil-free electricity, demand for fossil-electricity, when appropriately taxed, could be highly elastic (i.e. doubling the price of electricity might more than halve consumption of electricity, and very much more than halve the consumption of fossil electricity.)

[81] http://www.eia.doe.gov/cneaf/coal/quarterly/html/t1p01p1.html 2006.

[82] http://tonto.eia.doe.gov/dnav/ng/ng_sum_snd_dcu_nus_a.htm Production 2006, imports 2005.

[83] http://tonto.eia.doe.gov/dnav/pet/pet_sum_crdsnd_adc_mbbl_m.htm 2005.

[84] See Annex 6.

[85] *A comparative analysis of woody biomass and coal for electricity generation under various CO2 emission reductions and taxes*, J. Gan and C.T. Smith, Biomass and Bioenergy (2006) 30, pp 396-303.

[86] As noted in Chapter 2, the need to replace a high proportion of the energy and transport infrastructure, would appear to set the stage for a construction boom.

[87] *Heat: How to stop the Plane from Burning*, George Monbiot, Chapter 10.

[88] Conrad Black's wife is reputed to have once explained that really you have to have two (private) planes, "since however well you plan, the plane is always on the wrong continent".

[89] NYTimes, 9/26/2007. "Inspector Finds Broad Failures in Oil Program".

[90] For a fuller treatment of many of these topics, see *Heat: How to Stop the World from Burning*, George Monbiot, Chapter 7.

[91] Ibid, p.104 and http://www.worldbank.org/html/fpd/em/transmission/technology_abb.pdf

[92] *Hell and High Water, and what we should do*, Joseph Romm, p.192.

[93] http://www.theaircar.com/aboutmdi.html.

[94] http://www.gather.com/viewArticle.jsp?articleId=281474976997773

[95] *A High Speed Revolution*, Economist, 7/7/2007, p. 61.

[96] *Hell and High Water, and what we should do*, Joseph Romm, p.185

[97] *Economist, Technology Quarterly*, September 2007, p.6.

[98] *Getting wind farms off the ground*, Economist, 6/9/2007, Technical Quarterly, p. 3.

[99] *A cool concept*, Economist, 6/9/2007, Technical Quarterly, p 4.

[100] A dismaying characteristic of the Bush administration has been that it has worked to ensure that neither the public nor the private sector comes to grips with these problems.

[101] Most of the nitrogen used to create anhydrous ammonia is in any case withdrawn from the atmosphere.

[102] http://www.buildinggreen.com/features/flyash/appendixa.cfm. (0.43 billion tons of carbon).

[103] In the mid-1970s, scientists at the Univ. of California, Irvine identified CFCs as the major cause ozone depletion in the upper atmosphere; this was later confirmed by satellite studies. When CFCs are released into the atmosphere, they move via air currents to altitudes ranging from 15 to 25 mi (25–40 km). There, they are dissociated by ultraviolet light as given by the reaction: CF2Cl2

CF2Cl + Cl. The resulting free chlorine atoms (Cl) decompose ozone (O3) into oxygen (O2), Cl + O3 ClO + O2, and are regenerated by interaction with free oxygen atoms (O), ClO + O Cl + O2. When chlorine is regenerated, it is free to continue to break down other ozone molecules. This process continues for the atmospheric lifetime of the chlorine atom (one to two years), during which it destroys an average of 100,000 ozone molecules. Chlorine radicals are removed from the stratosphere after forming two compounds that are relatively resistant to dissociation by ultraviolet light: hydrogen chloride (HCl) and chlorine nitrate (ClONO2). Dissociation is slow enough so that these compounds can diffuse down to the troposphere, where they react with water vapor and are removed in rain.

[104] Progress even here may be less than it seems:

"In a hotel in Hangzou City, the Chinese trader swiftly got down to business. 'I have been supplying an Italian client with over 100 tons of CFCs with no problem,' he told the Western chemicals dealer. 'I can label the shipment as a different chemical if you are worried.' An hour later the two shook hands with mutual promises. The Chinese supplier had no idea his potential buyer was an EIA (Environmental Investigation Agency) investigator secretly filming the entire meeting." http://www.ecocrimes.com/global.html.

[105] http://www.afeas.org/greenhouse_gases.html.

[106] http://www.afeas.org/greenhouse_gases.html.

[107] *The Carbon Wars*, Jeremy Leggett, Routledge, 2001.

[108] NYTimes, May17, 2007, p.A17. See also www.archetecture2030.org.

[109] The basic rule seems to be "if you cannot tell the difference then it is the same" this has lead to the WTO being vilified by environmentalists and labor activists, who would like to see greater weight given to environmental damage, unsafe labor practices and health concerns.

[110] Newsweek, 5/16/2007, p. 94

[111] See for instance, "Oil Industry Says Biofuel Push May Keep Gas Prices High" (NYTimes, 5/24/2007), that reports industry uncertainty as to proposed ethanol supplies is holding back investment in new refineries, and thus causing shortages and higher gas prices. In this case, and viewed from a global warming perspective, uncertainly is beneficial, but it would be better to be clear that government policy ensures that any new investment in refining capacity is likely to be unprofitable.

[112] Earlier in his speech, he outlines steps to decrease American dependence on imported oil, but this was an oil-dependence policy, not an environmental/global warming policy. Indeed some of the alternative fuel proposals seemed to contain the seeds of increased, rather than decreased use of fossil fuels.

[113] Thus an email from Barbara Boxer of 8/2/2007 said "Last weekend, I led a delegation of 10 Senators on a trip to Greenland to take a first-hand look at the devastating effects of global warming. Words like 'awesome,' 'majestic,' and 'incredible' don't go far enough to describe what we saw as our boat rode alongside icebergs as large as coliseums. These icebergs -- average age 9,000 years -- have broken off an ice stream and are now melting at an astonishing rate. The entire Greenland ice sheet is 1200 miles long by 500 miles wide and, unless we act now, this melting will lead to a catastrophic rise in sea levels.

That's why it's so critical that we act -- now -- to stop global warming." Unfortunately Senate Bill 306 *The Global Warming Reduction Act,* being sponsored by Senator Boxer provides for cap and trade, not a revenue neutral carbon tax. Much better than nothing, but if passed cap and trade should be replaced by a carbon tax at the earliest opportunity.

[114] The impact on global temperature from whatever source, sun, orbit, CO2, aerosols, etc.

[115] *The Rough Guide to Climate Change*, Robert Henson, p. 229.

[116] The IPCC models usually calculate sensitivity at the equilibrium temperature at 550 ppm. Given the approximations involved 560 vs 550 ppm lies well within the range of error.

[117] Dr. Hansen has factored in other greenhouse gasses, 'black soot' and sulfate-aerosols, so fortunately his estimate is likely to be more reliable than the simplistic calculations in Table 7. However, it is interesting to see that "back of the envelope" calculations also lead to the conclusion that we have no time to waste.

[118] Hansen, *Political interference with government climate change science*, 19 March 2007 testimony to Committee on Oversight and Government Reform of the U.S. House of Representatives, http://www.columbia.edu/~jeh1.

[119] *Permanent carbon dioxide storage in deep-sea sediments*, House et al., Proc. Natl. Acad. Sci., 103, 12291-12295)

[120] *Air Pollution Workshop,* West et al., 2005, www.giss.nasa.gov/meetings/pollution2005.

[121] *Auto Chiefs Make Headway Against a Mileage Increase*, NYTimes, 6/7/2007, p C1.

[122] As of this writing (9/30/2007) Congressman John Dingell, Chairman of the House Energy and Commerce Committee has introduced draft carbon legislation. Key provisions call for carbon tax of $50.00 per ton, introduced over 5 years (i.e. in $10.00 per ton annual increments) and an additional 50 cent/gallon tax on gasoline (and aviation spirits). Clearly a step in the right direction, this still falls well short of the *$250 ton* of carbon tax introduced **NOW**, recommended

in this book. Chairman Dingell goes half way towards revenue neutrality with significant increases in the Earned Income Credit, with the balance ear-marked for "good causes", http://www.house.gov/dingell/carbonTaxSummary.shtml

[123] The nature of the problem, and the answer have been known in the right academic circles since 1992:

"The corrective nature of pollution charges provides a "double dividend": a revenue-neutral tax policy change, combining the introduction of pollution charges with the reduction or elimination of other taxes, would both protect the environment by reducing by reducing harmful emissions and offset market distortions associated with other taxes (for example, US personal and corporate income taxes generate distortions or pure losses of 20 to 50 cents for every new dollar of revenue collected). This double dividend may be particularly relevant in today's political climate where policy makers are reluctant to consider any new taxes." *Pollution Charges for Environmental Protection: A Policy Link Between Energy and the Environment*, R. Stavins and B. Whitehead, Annual Review of Energy and the Environment, 17: 187-210, 1992.

[124] This is a typical Bush baffle you statement. We get no clue as to what technological breakthrough he is anticipating.

[125] www.commondreams.org/headlines06/1016-01.htm

[126] http://www.wnd.com/news/article.asp?ARTICLE_ID=54528

billhobbs.com/2007/02/more_on_gore.html

[127] *Hell and High Water, and what we should do.* p.224.

[128] http://www.luntzspeak.com/graphics/NewYorkTimes.NewsStory.pdf and http://www.luntzspeak.com/graphics/NewYorkTimes.Editorial.pdf.

[129] http://www.youtube.com/watch?v=4Yz8UwRsWPA

[130] *The Great Leap Backward?* , Elizabeth C. Economy, *Foreign Affairs,Sept/Oct2007.*

[131] April 25, 2007.

[132] Steve Running, IPCC WG2 Lead Author Chapter 14, "North America" (Professor, Department of Ecosystem Sciences, University of Montana). http://www.sciencedaily.com/releases/2007/04/070406111556.htm

[133] http://marketplace.publicradio.org/shows/2007/01/30/PM200701305.html

[134] Gary Yohe, IPCC WG2 Coordinating Lead Author Chapter 20, "Perspectives on Climate Change and Sustainability" (Woodhouse/Sysco Professor of Economics, Wesleyan University). http://www.sciencedaily.com/releases/2007/04/070406111556.htm

[135] http://www.sciencedaily.com/releases/2007/04/070406111556.htm, emphasis added.

[136] This book has been at pains to distinguish between fossil and bio-carbon, arguing that it is *additions* of fossil carbon (or more generally fossil greenhouse gasses) to the natural carbon cycle, that are the major cause of global warming. However, it is clear that the natural carbon cycle involves major sequestration of carbon within the cycle, forests, methane hydrate and permafrost to mention three. If global warming triggers release of carbon from these sequestered sinks, this could lead to a significant jump in atmospheric CO_2 (or greenhouse gasses) and associated temperature rise and harmful climatic impacts.

[137] *Lamps replaced and alternative vehicles bought, but battle over coal plants remains*, Associated Press, 6/11/2007.

[138] Senate Democrats Propose Loans for Coal-Based Fuel Plants, NYTimes, 6/13/2007.

[139] The Christian Science Monitor, 5/22/2007.

[140] *Hell and High Water, and what we should do*, Joseph Romm, p232.

[141] http://www.ecobusinesslinks.com/carbon_offset_wind_credits_carbon_reduction.htm

[142] But bio-carbon and bio-methane are not an "air pollutant", emphasis added.

[143] http://www.fueleconomy.gov/feg/co2.shtml

[144] http://tonto.eia.doe.gov/FTPROOT/petroleum/caprice.pdf

[145] Cost structures for energy from fossil fuels are not easily available. "The purpose of the escape valve is to limit harm from unexpectedly high costs that might arise if the emission limit is tightened too fast, by putting a ceiling on marginal cost. To keep the emission limit meaningful, however, the escape valve price should be set high enough that it is relatively unlikely to be reached: a suitable initial value might be $75 to $100 per ton of carbon, equivalent to about 18 to 24 cents per gallon of gasoline or 0.8 to 2.4 cents.KwH of electricity, depending on fuel source", *The Science and Politics of Global Climate Change: A Guide to the Debate.* Andrew Dessler and Edward Parsons, p.160.

[146] http://www.energy.ca.gov/gasoline/whats_in_barrel_oil.html

[147] IPCC GCM runs no longer use a BAU scenario, however the A2 scenario used in the results we report here is the closest to BAU of those considered.

A multimodel ensemble approach to assessment of climate change impacts on the hydrology and water resources of the Colorado River basin, N. Christensen and D. P. Lettenmaier, Department of Civil and Environmental Engineering Box 352700, University of Washington, Seattle WA 98195, USA.

[148] http://www.grida.no/climate/ipcc/emission/030.htm

[149] http://www.grida.no/climate/ipcc/emission/data/allscen.htm

[150]***

Global CO2 Emissions from Fossil-Fuel Burning,   ***

*** Cement Manufacture, and Gas Flaring: 1751-2003   ***

***   ***

*** May 30, 2006   ***

***   ***

*** Source: Gregg Marland   ***

***   Bob Andres   ***

***   Tom Boden   ***

***   Carbon Dioxide Information Analysis Center   ***

***   Oak Ridge National Laboratory   ***

***   Oak Ridge, Tennessee 37831-6335   ***

****

All emission estimates are expressed in million metric tons of carbon.

Per capita emission estimates are expressed in metric tons of carbon.

Population estimates were not available to permit calculations of global per capita estimates before 1950. Please note that annual sums were tallied before each element (e.g., Gas) was rounded and reported here so totals may differ slightly from the sum of the elements due to rounding.

http://cdiac.ornl.gov/ftp/ndp030/global.1751_2003.ems

[151] Multigas Greenhouse Gases Emissions in a Computable General Equilibrium Model.,Elisa Lanzi, School of Advanced Studies in Venice, Italy, http://www. feem-web.it/ess06/files/lanzi-fp.pdf